Indispensables
of Piano Playing

Indispensables

of

Piano

Playing

ABBY WHITESIDE

CHARLES SCRIBNER'S SONS   NEW YORK

Printed in the United States of America
Library of Congress Catalog Card Number 61-18671

Second Edition

To my pupil friends

Contents

Foreword

Teaching has been an exciting experience since I squarely faced the unpleasant fact, more than twenty-five years ago, that the pupils in my studio played or didn't play, and that was that. The talented ones progressed, the others didn't—and I could do nothing about it.

This fact became a challenge which forced me to disbelieve in the tools I was using and led me to discoveries which mean that all can play. By virtue of the principle which has been established and the teaching techniques I have been able to develop since that day when I really came to grips with the problem, the less gifted can learn as well as the most gifted.

From the outset I demanded of myself, as the only sure proof I was coming to the right conclusions, that I learn to play the difficult Chopin Etudes at top speed. It took me twenty years to learn to play the Octave Etude, Op. 25, No. 10. All that signifies is that it took me twenty years, through my own study of this Etude in particular and through experiment with many pupils, to become sufficiently aware of faulty habits to achieve a clear analysis of the mechanics which are involved in playing the piano. The fun of playing and the realization of beautiful music appear only when the free play of the intricate mechanism for handling the instrument is governed by, and infused with, a controlling, encompassing rhythm.

The experience of teaching a professional violinist, one who has played the literature since he was fourteen years old but didn't like his performance (violin—not piano, and teaching— not coaching—which means that I dealt always with the mechanics of playing as well as with the musical results), has furnished concrete proof that there is a principle which holds for all learning of skills. I do not play the violin, but it became evident to me, almost from the start of my work with him, that the violinist's problems—principles of using power and distance —were identical with the problems I deal with daily in teaching my piano students. It was also apparent that his listening habits, as regards the musical statement, were conditioned by his physical habits of producing tone. After fifteen months, all the things he has always wanted begin to sound in the music he produces.

No factual analysis of what takes place in a beautiful performance can be complete. I can only hope that this book, by noting factors and actions involved, may help to clarify the picture; and that, by suggesting ways and means of using a rhythm, it may simplify the whole learning of the skill.

I am deeply grateful and indebted to my pupils who have shared this whole search for a simpler means to implement the learning of this skill of piano playing. Without their help this book would never have been written.

Special gratitude goes to Stanley Baron, who prepared the manuscript. I also wish to thank Roger Boardman, Marion Flagg, and Joseph Prostakoff for their criticism and suggestions.

A. W.

Abby Whiteside, author of *Indispensables of Piano Playing,* was teaching, making new discoveries, jotting down ideas and illustrations up to the very end of her life.

'I'his book contains the synthesis of her piano teaching, developed over a period of almost fifty years. Her first book, *The Pianist's Mechanism,* published in 1929 (G. Schirmer), marks her earliest efforts to find more effective teaching tools. After completing *Indispensables of Piano Playing,* she began working on a study dealing with the performing problems of the Chopin Etudes. Although this manuscript is incomplete, she did formulate her main ideas. This work is scheduled for future publication by the Abby Whiteside Foundation, which has been established since her death, by former pupils and friends.

Indispensables of Piano Playing was a peculiarly difficult book to write because Abby Whiteside's principles and methods of instruction dealt so much with *physical sensation.* No one who ever worked with her needs to be reminded of the extraordinary skill she had in creating this physical awareness of a proper adjustment. Once achieved, there was infinitely more than a merely intellectual comprehension of what she said. She was endowed with one of the prime requirements for a piano teacher: extreme, indeed, exquisite sensitivity of muscular control. What was more, she had taught herself to transfer some of this inordinately subtle awareness to her pupils. Sensation always came first: words were secondary. It is remarkable how much she was able to crystallize in her writing in spite of the subtleties she was dealing with, which by their very nature were resistant to verbal expression.

Abby Whiteside understood the importance of pedagogy. She knew the difficulties of getting a meaningful musical education, for she herself had had to abandon all she had ever been taught and start all over again in search of basic principles. Because she had singleness of mind, tenacity, originality, a deep love for the piano, and, above all, more than a touch of genius, she achieved her goal. She was unique among the piano teachers of her time in knowing exactly what made the playing mechanism function, for she started from nature it-self — from a study of anatomy and its application to the complex skill of playing the piano.

Every chapter of this book has its special importance for the pianist and the piano teacher, but its focus is precisely where Abby Whiteside intended it to be: in her treatment of basic rhythm. She supported her statements with concrete illus-trations. The reader must read and reread the text, test the illustrations, and, above all, must seek to become physically aware of its significance; for Abby Whiteside's concept of a basic body rhythm is the foundation of her approach. Without it there can never be facility and beauty in performance.

The book is a very personal statement. Those who had the good fortune to know this remarkable woman can almost hear her voice as they read it. It represents the fruit of con-tinuous experimentation and objective assessment — as elab-orate and painstaking as any research that is conducted in a laboratory. No one else in the piano field, performer or teacher, has ever studied or written about the skill and its problems in this particular way.

Now that Abby Whiteside is gone, this text has taken on a new and enhanced value, leading any searching and aspiring pianist into a whole new world of ease, expertness, and musical sensitivity, making this book more than ever "Indispensable."

October 1961

Marion Flagg   Sophia Rosoff
Joseph Prostakoff   Stanley Baron

Indispensables
of Piano Playing

I   Author's Premise

For the purposes of this introductory chapter, let me reduce the business of playing the piano to its simplest terms. We begin, let us say, with a person who has feeling for music, who loves its sounds and wishes to reproduce them. The beauty of music being in the ear, the problem is this: how to transfer what is a bodiless aural image into the ultimate contact of fingers against a keyboard of black and white keys.

The answer is that this transfer must somehow be all of a piece, it must be centrally controlled by the aural image, it must be cohesive. It is the body *as a whole* which transfers the *idea* of music into the actual production of music.

An exciting rhythm, a unifying, all-encompassing rhythm is

the *only* possible means by which the entire playing mechanism (which consists of the muscles of the arm, the bony structure of the hand, and the fingers) can be brought into full play. A basic rhythm is the *only* possible over-all coordinator, for it is not merely the instigator of beautiful musical production, but it is the sole factor that can successfully translate the image in the ear and the emotion which must be at the bottom of all beautiful music into a function of the whole body.

The problems of the pianist must not be too sharply differentiated from those of the dancer, the singer, the violinist. Indeed, all bodily skills (not only those concerned with music) have this in common: they always involve the *whole* body if the best results are to be obtained. The body is the *center* of all these skills, even though in each case there is a necessary *periphery* of some kind involved. In the instance of the pianist this periphery is, of course, the actual contact of fingers against the keys. But the one fact which must be repeated incessantly, because so many mistakes have been made on this score, is that the center controls the periphery; it can never be the other way around. The body governs the fingers in playing the piano, and no amount of coaching in finger dexterity will ever lead to the easy beauty in playing that must be our objective. The fingers in themselves have no power of coordination. The *body* must be taught, and the fingers will find their way under the guidance of this central control.

Nothing must ever be allowed to interrupt the flow of a long-line rhythm, for only the rhythm can encompass the statement of musical ideas. Movements of articulation, such as finger action on the keys and the position of the wrists, must never impede the full musical statement. In themselves, movements of articulation can never express musical ideas or emotions. *In themselves,* they can never reproduce the unique beauty of musical conception and form which is contained in the ear. Like the dancer's leg movements, like the baseball player's bat or the golfer's club, the pianist's fingers are the outermost parts of a mechanism which cannot function to the best advantage without a central control. A fundamental rhythm is this control.

Teaching should therefore be concerned primarily with stimulating, cultivating and preserving a heightened sense of rhythm. That is the major, almost the only, purpose of teaching this skill.

Routine drill is a poor substitute for the fun of utilizing ears and rhythm for making music—a process in which the necessary technique performs its function without being noticed. The best possible procedure is to interfere as little as possible with nature's manner of using power. That means a coordination from center to periphery. It cannot happen from periphery to center.

The hand is equipped with a bony structure which can easily transmit the power of the large muscles for tone production. Therein lies its real efficiency. Training the hand first and separately for the delivery of power establishes habits of action at the periphery which block a coordination from center to periphery.

Systematically working to develop finger-hitting power is worse than simply a waste of time. Its by-product is the establishment of habits of tone production which tend to blot out the vivid awareness that a surging rhythm is what makes the music shine.

The inevitable result of training fingers for tone production is the conditioning of listening habits to a note-wise procedure, and this is probably more destructive even than the pain of neuritis, which can and often does result from strain.

A note-wise procedure can cause havoc in the full development of powers. It can slow up the process of learning repertoire, and trespasses on a continuing rhythm. A note-wise procedure ties the music down to a labored progression because it does not automatically highlight important tones; more important, it literally destroys the possibility of developing one's potential gifts for musical perception.

A note-wise procedure can never produce a phrase of supreme beauty.

When there is absolute pitch, a note-wise procedure may intensify all these faults—which means that it very frequently damages the highly gifted aural learners more than the average talent. With separate initiations of power by fingers, acute pitch perception reduces the listening to the the's, and's and but's of the music.

A note-wise procedure cannot further a blended action of all the potentials for taking distance and furnishing the power for tone.

A technique which encompasses the difficulties of the instrument must utilize the principle that a repeated action by a large lever can absorb actions by smaller levers. The continuity in action of this repetition by the large lever should not be interrupted by the action of the smaller levers. This is essential for a fluent technique. It is also a requisite for swinging down the line of musical form, when the repetition by the large levers is reserved for important tones, and the musical modifiers are tucked in on the way by the smaller levers.

Nothing less than the entire body can furnish the control for a real rhythm, for the most delicate gradations in the use of dynamics, for the most powerful climaxes.

All training, to be efficient, must never lose sight of the fact that it is the output of the body as a whole which develops the full potentialities of the player.

Only a basic rhythm can coordinate the body as a whole.

Rhythm

The performer *feels* the rhythm of the music and listens to the tones.

Feeling the rhythm is one half of a beautiful performance. The other half is the aural image of the music.

This is a grossly simplified statement, but very good imagery for sensing the importance of the role played by a rhythm. This rhythm started music on its way. Rhythm is the most potent of all the forces which influence listening habits. Rhythm channels the emotional surge which the music creates if the piano is beautifully played. Rhythm is the only possible coordinator for expert timing. It is a simple and very adequate tool for developing the feeling for form. Rhythm is the core of the blended activity of the entire playing mechanism.

Rhythm is also the basis of good sight reading. It produces the measured slowness which makes fast playing beautiful—something more than just being fast. It is an absolute necessity for simplicity in projecting musical ideas. It deserves being dealt with as a factor which creates magic, for it can dissolve all technical problems until they lose their identity in its current. It works in the simplest possible fashion in spite of the fact that it has been cluttered up and very nearly buried in a welter of loose talk concerning its origin and operation.

Rhythm stems from the point of resistance to the application of power. It creates its magic by a follow-through activity which involves a balancing of weight of the entire body. The point of resistance when we are on our feet is the floor; when we are seated it is the chair seat.

We do not need any teaching to understand that it is not the application of power to the ice through one foot after another that creates the thrill in skating. We simply feel the thrill of the balancing and swaying of the body, and a permeating exhilaration results from this coordinated movement.

If we are skating to music the ears are involved. They dictate the timing of the push-offs so that the swaying and balancing of the body may fit the music. A rude interruption of that synchronization of the physical imagery with the music is unpleasant and we instinctively avoid it by not being out of step with the musical push-offs—the important beats.

This synchronization of the push-offs with the music, which creates the follow-through activity that brings about the swaying and pleasure in skating, should be the *same*, not different, for the pianist. The push-offs are the action of the top arm taking control of important tones, and this action by the upper arm should always be indissolubly linked with the torso. That is, the torso, which contacts resistance at the chair seat with the ischial bones, and is the fulcrum which makes the power of the top arm effective, never sits back stodgily and lets the arm do the work, as it were. Rather, the torso is so vitally balanced that it participates in all the actions of the arm, and creates an outlet for the emotional response to the music.

Never lose sight of the fact that playing the piano involves two very definite operations: application of power to the key (vertical action) and progression along the keyboard (horizontal action). The music itself possesses two definite attributes: the details, and the ideas as a whole.

There must be a physical activity which sets up the horizontal progression just as well as the activity which takes care of the vertical key-drop. Just as emphatically there must be a physical activity which sets up the phrase as a whole, as well as the activity which produces the details.

Leave out the physical activity which belongs to the phrase-wise procedure and we have left only the physical activity which belongs to a note-wise procedure—exactly what happens in all ugly piano playing.

The physical activity which sets up a phrase-wise procedure has its inception in the top arm. If only piano playing emphasized and demanded a rhythmic balancing—so necessary in skating to avoid a mishap—the beauty in output would be greatly increased. There is no more possibility of relating performance in piano playing to important musical push-offs and creating a beautiful line without a related physical push-off and follow-through, than there is in skating. It must be there. Watch for the presence of this rhythmic activity of top arm and torso, instead of watching hand position and finger activity, if you want to learn about a long-line rhythm.

Just so long as the achieving of a playing skill is believed to be related solely to the mechanical drill of levers instead of to the one gigantic spring which feeds all the controls—a rhythm—there will be a multitude of players who never glimpse the source of a thrilling performance.

The one factor, aside from the aural image, which could insure the development of all potential capacity is practically never the starting point with teachers. Not only is it rarely the starting point (which unquestionably it should be), but it almost never gets to be the all-important point; and thus we have all the frustration and misery which are all too frequently the lot of many gifted young players.

It is right here that we need to heed the procedure and results of the talented jazz pianists. They have a tune in their ears and a rhythm in their bodies, and they let these two elements fuse by using nothing else as they learn their instrument. They do not fuss with hand position, fingering, learning to read straight off, learning to count, before they produce a rhythmic tune. Once the rhythmic tune is accomplished, nothing can stop them from having fun with it. They embellish it and in so doing learn to play.

It is not that simple for the less gifted who may wish to play with just as overwhelming an urge; but that is no reason for blocking them by thrusting all the less important factors at them in the beginning. What logic is there in using the least productive tools for the less gifted?

Unless we learn to use the same tools in teaching which the gifted players use instinctively if let alone, we certainly are substituting intellectual concepts for nature's manner of learning. And no theory can be valid that clutters up the learning process with factors which rate a low second in importance.

The factors of first importance must be dealt with first. This can mean nothing for the potential pianist but the development of sensitive listening through the use of a fundamental rhythm, and letting these two factors become indissolubly fused for making music.

The orchestra is a wonderful place for observing this fundamental rhythm and the manner in which it channels the emotional response to the music. You can pick out the first-chair men by their swaying bodies as well as by listening to their lilting phrases. These men are full of rhythm and feeling for the music. That is the reason they are first-chair men, and because they are seated this rhythm and emotion find outlet in the balanced activity of arms and a swaying torso.

Just imagine any of the orchestra men getting excited and expressing that excitement through the actions which govern pitch. It is true that their pitch and power for tone are not produced in the same place. It is also true that the excitement influences the use of their power without interfering with the action for producing pitch. But even so, can you imagine a like phrase in beauty being produced unless the excitement of the playing has a chance to be linked with a power which can be related to phrase-wise production? Getting excited and having no channel for expressing that excitement, except with a hitting or fingering process, means sheer mutilation to a phrase-wise procedure.

For the pianist there must be a rhythm somewhere other than in the hitting process. It can easily happen with the push-offs, with top arm plus the torso. Then the pianist, too, can control phrase-wise modeling with the magic of a rhythm which absorbs key hitting.

A primary difficulty in piano playing is making this physical relationship realistic and clearly identifiable. But that is only because there is a welter of established methods dealing with proper ways of hitting the keys, and no such preponderance of emphasis on how to deal with and develop an emotional rhythm. Even when key hitting does not have any relation to the production of dynamics, as in the case of the harpsichord or the organ, it still receives all too much emphasis. And the activity which deals with creating a fundamental rhythm—top arms and the activity against chair seat—isn't recognized as a crucial factor in playing. Yet, only this fundamental rhythm can create a spacing between tones which produces a phrase that is breathtaking in its beauty.

This kind of spacing cannot be produced by the ear alone; even the best of ears are insufficient. Spacing involves a timing of action of the sort which develops world's-record makers in the field of sports. There is always a follow-through in rhythmic progression which absorbs and governs all the complexities in action.

The projection of the musical idea must of necessity be related to the rhythm of form if there is to be simplicity in the musical statement; and simplicity in statement is a first requisite of the professional performer. Unless the audience can listen easily without confusion, they simply do not listen. As the organ is all too frequently played there is very little simplicity. Effects are produced by mechanical devices and nothing but a masterful rhythm can so synchronize all the actions necessary to produce color and dynamics that the instrument is played with simplicity. Let a great artist handle the organ and there is not a hint of the mechanics of the instrument; there is only phrase-modeling of rare beauty. There is a helpful illustration in organ playing of the relation of a balanced torso to a keyboard instrument. Both arms and legs must have full freedom of action, and the torso balanced against the organ bench furnishes the player with the necessary equilibrium.

As another example, the juggler exhibits a never-ending rhythm with perfection in timing. He may keep ten articles in the air at one time. He throws and catches with his arms and hands, while his body furnishes the rhythmic progression. It is the alertness of the body as a whole which makes his perfection possible.

The pianist needs this same fluidity in balanced action for his rhythm; but, because there is not the same demand for it in simply manipulating the instrument, it is all too often ignored or not understood.

The most convincing illustration of the effect of this rhythm upon performance is the difference in the way in which the same pianist will play when under the domination of the rhythm of an orchestra and when he is in a solo concert. The performer is a gifted, sensitive person. He is incapable of ignoring the rhythm of the orchestra; he gets involved in its sweep and, in so doing, his entire output is changed. He is swept along inside the current of this rhythm and it makes for inspired playing. Alone, he is the victim of his practicing habits. If these habits are not those of practicing to perfect an emotional rhythm, then he is concentrating largely on details. Consequently his performance will deal too largely with details; he will linger in the wrong places, and he will almost surely have far too many climaxes. That is, his faulty practice perfects everything but the emotional rhythm. The net result is an uninspired performance.

One could easily make a list of the pianists who can be counted upon to play well with an orchestra, but who are sure to fail in solo performance. This list would not, of course, include the names of the truly great artists. They always command the situation and never do anything but create music, whether with the orchestra or without. And always, in their case, a fundamental rhythm is the physical counterpart of the aural image, taking care of details and making them beautiful but never allowing them to do anything else except to contribute to the performance as a whole. They all exhibit this tremendous rhythmic force; they play by it, they are saturated with it—and thus it is that we, the audience, are thrilled by a creative performance of astonishing beauty.

In this kind of performance there is always a slow, easy, graceful rhythm even in fast playing. Without this rhythm, fast playing is spectacular for speed but not for beauty.

One hears stories from men who have played under Toscanini to the effect that they have surpassed themselves in their playing. Why? Because there is no stopping the rhythmic current when Toscanini holds the baton. He is a dynamo of rhythmic energy when he conducts, and that rhythm permeates every man under him. They play as if they were possessed, as indeed they are, of a new facility and power. That compelling rhythm taps a hidden source of ability, brushing aside any undue emphasis on this or that. Nature has taken over. The rhythm forces the issue and the result becomes a blended co-ordination, right for virtuosity of a higher order than could not be possible unless a rhythm of that sort was fairly intoxicating the performer.

Feats in sight reading are accomplished only by people who work under the spell of a rhythm. I have been told of an orchestra that was rehearsing a contemporary score of great difficulty. There were multiple changes in meter and no one was getting the feel of the music except the flutist. When the men asked him how he did it, he replied, "Well, I couldn't count the stuff so I just got a rhythm in my body and kept it going."

If only we could absorb that very fundamental and revealing truth we would constantly use the only productive technical means for learning to read music and play our instrument.

Put a rhythm in your body and keep it going.

There is nothing vague or complicated in that statement. There is nothing vague or complicated in the activity which puts the rhythm in the body for the pianist, any more than for the flutist or the skater.

The activity of the top arm, augmented by the activity against the chair seat—and both related to the important tones of the music, like the push-offs of the skater related to the musical push-offs—create the swaying, the follow-through, the feeling of rhythm in the body.

Observe this follow-through activity which is the result of the push-offs. Once it is created, it becomes creative—in a magical and unbelievable manner. It stretches the listening; it intensifies the feeling for the musical idea as a whole. It does this by a slow, intense, controlled action somewhere in the body. No one can dictate this activity. All that should be done is to make the player aware of all possible activities which create a physical response in the torso (as well as top arm) to the music which is being played.

If that seems difficult to accept, try it. Not once, but always, when a pupil experiences this relation of torso activity to the activity for tone production, it is a revelation to him. Such phrases as "I have never heard it that way before," "The page does not even look the same," "Oh, now I know what you have been talking about," "I never felt a rhythm until my body began to sway," have expressed the surprise in achievement.

Nowhere in the piano literature is the demand for this rhythm more demonstrable than in the playing of a Beethoven Sonata. Only the artists who have it ever produce an electrifying performance of Op. 111 or, for that matter, any of the Sonatas.

I do not mean to infer that a fundamental rhythm alone can produce a magnificent performance of Op. 111, if the player lacks the capacity for creative ideas and emotional intensity. But the fact remains that only the follow-through of a basic rhythm can channel the ideas and emotions so that there can be the subtlety in the use of dynamics and rhythmic nuance necessary for a great performance of Beethoven. Not only does it channel ideas. When it permeates the entire being of a musician, then and then only is there growth and output in ideas which fulfill the early indications of talent.

Other than ears, this rhythm is almost the sole arbiter of what is called "musical maturity" in performance. If that is too strong a statement, then it is certainly the one greatest factor in the *development* of "musical maturity."

To establish a follow-through activity in the total physical production for playing is certainly a simple manner in which to gain a most cherished result. It is one of the truly amazing attributes of a rhythm that it can accomplish results, easily and often instantaneously, which have been unattainable when it was not motivating the form. We shall never know enough about this magical rhythm, but certainly the only way of learning more and more is to give it the place of honor in learning to play our instrument.

There is no complication in establishing this follow-through with the total mechanism of arms and torso unless there are already established habits of using the shoulder girdle and arms as a unit, rhythmically unrelated to the lower part of the torso. This lifting and holding of the shoulders is not infrequently an expression of the emotional response. It is also a frequent cause of strain and pain between the shoulder blades.

Learning to bounce the torso by contracting the muscles of the buttocks uses a definite control of those muscles, which makes one easily aware of an activity which does proceed from base and follow-through. Also, the bouncing of the torso in this manner creates an activity which easily enhances the gaiety of dance forms, as related to tone production of the top arm; and always the activity of the torso has its greatest value when it expresses emotion. If the emotions run amuck, the beauty of form is distorted. Running amuck can mean only one thing for the pianist: that he becomes involved emotionally with the activity controlling articulation rather than with the activity producing a rhythm.

It is most unfortunate that the movements which express emotion are labeled mannerisms, for we think of mannerisms as unnecessary. If they are always present with a great performance can they be unnecessary? Rather, isn't it safer to believe that they *are* necessary for the expression of the emotion which must be a part of any great performance?

There should be no prejudice against so-called mannerisms. We should just be thankful for the emotion which vivifies and heightens the output of a creative artist. There is far too much playing which is merely glib—lacking in any real emotional output—*real* in the sense that it enhances the beauty of performance and does not distort it.

Only this emotional follow-through of the rhythm can make the use of dynamics so volatile and fluctuating that they register the most delicate whimsy of the aural image.

The block to realizing the magic of this rhythm is created by the listening habits conditioned by and related to a finger technique. The block will disappear as the follow-through of a rhythm appears with greater and greater persistence in its control.

Here is a story of just such a taking over by a rhythm:

Mr. A was coming up for an examination for a master's degree in music education. The piano was one of his minors. He was failing in it and in dictation. One day his clever teacher asked him if he could play any jazz. He answered, "Oh yes, I can play simple jazz by ear if I have heard it a few times." Yet, when he sat in a class and was asked to take dictation he failed. When he tried to learn a simple Bach Minuet it was a baffling ordeal. His applied learning had no relation to his natural use of ears and rhythm. When it was suggested that the process should be identical, that Bach should be as rhythmic as jazz, he lost his halting procedure and passed his examinations without difficulty.

The net result of starting and continuing to learn with this basic rhythmic follow-through is progress which is rapid to the point of astonishment with a talented pupil, and progress which far outstrips any former achievements for the less talented.

The feeling of rhythmic progression can become so dominant when linked to the emotional surge that it fairly sucks the details of the music into its current. This kind of intensity in musical progression dissipates the effect of bar lincs, which all too frequently become a major hurdle in achieving grace of form.

It is an interesting contradiction that the bar lines which, for the composer, are entirely associated with harmonic and structural progression, become a hazard for the performer. That is only because the performer builds up the vicious habit of making interruptions of bar lines when the all-encompassing rhythm related from the first tone to the last of a musical idea is not the primary motivation of the activity in performance.

3 Difficulties Peculiar to the Piano

The moment we accept the fact that the pianist cannot control tone quality, and that the nature of tone production does not demand continuity in power, we are confronted in a startling manner with the fact that the peculiar difficulties of our instrument are musical ones. In order to influence tone quality in an instrument the performer's tone-producing energy must contact the vibrator which produces the pitch. In the case of the piano, a felt hammer hits a string—the vibrator. The performer applies his power to a key. The key action trips the hammer which strikes the string. The performer can only make the hammer hit with greater or less force. There are percussive noises in playing the piano and these noises vary according to the manner of delivering power to the key. But these noises are not the tone, and one should differentiate between them and tone.

A precise delivery of energy, aiming to release the power just before the keybed resistance is reached, will diminish the thud against the keybed. Being unaware of this level for focusing energy for tone allows one to jam against the keybed with great force.

Since there is no control over the quality of tone, the pianist is left with rhythm and dynamics for expressing the feeling for the music, while the instruments using breath or bow have rhythm, dynamics and color quality. It pays to be realistic in this matter; it adds to our awareness of the tremendous importance of rhythm and dynamics in projecting a musical idea.

Then when we see that by the nature of tone production—applying the energy to the key—there is no actual demand made of the pianist for a continuity in physical action that produces a rhythmic follow-through, we are brought up against the fact that the piano does not demand a rhythm even in order to hit all the keys accurately.

Yet it is a rhythm which is the all-encompassing factor in dealing with dynamics. Dynamics do not control a rhythm, but certainly a rhythm does control the subtle use of dynamics. It is here that we face the most important problem in mastering the piano: the making of a rhythm the primary factor. This it certainly must be in acquiring facility and beauty in performance, since it is not a demanded factor by the nature of tone production.

Without a fundamental rhythm there can be no expert timing, which is a basic requirement for perfection in any feat of dexterity, be it piano or sport.

Without a fundamental rhythm no piano playing can ever rate better than second-class.

It is unfortunate for the pianist that there is not the same demand for a balanced activity in learning to play that there is for the ice-skater in learning his skill. The skater must deal constantly with a rhythmic balance until it is achieved, or else be subject to dangerous falls. Not so in piano playing. We can plod along with no rhythmic grace, hitting one key and then another, and in so doing never achieve that undulating rhythm which alone is adequate for the mastery of mechanics as well as full musical development.

This is the monumental difficulty of the piano: it does not itself further the achievement of a physical continuity in action.

We have two opposing directions to deal with in playing the piano: progression along the horizontal keyboard, and the vertical key action which receives the power for tone. The continuity in action, which is the basis of a long-line rhythm, can only be established in the movement of the upper arm, plus the action of the torso, which is the fulcrum for the application of power by the arm. The arm is connected to the torso by a circular joint with an extraordinary capacity for allowing several things to happen simultaneously. No matter what the movement of the upper arm may be, that movement is integrated with the torso so that the torso is actually a part—an associated action—of the upper arm.

Even when there is not a horizontal progression, which means a shift of position of the hand along the keyboard, there is a span of time which is related to the progression of the music. This span of time can and should be filled in with activity of the upper arm plus torso, which is the expression of the feeling for a phrase-wise procedure.

The relationships formed in the handling of these directions —the basic rhythm to the actions of articulation—have resulted in using the words "horizontal" and "vertical" to highlight the physical actions as related to the musical output. Saying, "The vertical actions have destroyed the horizontal progression," means the playing has lost its sensitivity. There is too much noise and too little grace. But it also means instantly that there is a physical relationship in activity which needs adjustment. "Not enough horizontal to carry the form." "Time between tones should be filled in with movements controlling horizontal progression, not with the vertical movements controlling articulation."

It is in this relation of horizontal to vertical actions—long-line rhythm to articulation—that the terms "legato" (connected) and "staccato" (detached) have caused difficulty rather than assistance in the pianist's phrase modeling. Since legato and staccato are indubitably linked in our minds with beautiful phrase modeling there needs to be a qualifying understanding of their actual operation for the pianist.

The term legato has been extended, as it is used in the case of tone production by breath or bow, to include a controlled fluctuation of dynamics with the holding process. With the possibility of controlled dynamics while holding the tone, the holding process becomes an expression of emotional intensity to the performer. Not so with the piano—it allows no such control. The tone diminishes in intensity immediately after it is sounded. Therefore if the pianist expressed any emotion through the holding process (unfortunately he frequently does), the result is merely a pressure against the keybed which in no way influences the held tone. This holding is worse than ineffectual. It stops the rhythm and destroys the possibility of the greatest subtlety in the use of dynamics. The pianist's phrases are modeled with dynamics at the inception of tone— and nothing but an exciting, progressing rhythm is adequate for the modeling.

So the pianist's legato needs to be concerned with horizontal progression, and in so doing can intensify the comprehensive rhythm which channels the emotions in a productive, not a wasteful, manner—productive in the sense that the modeling with dynamics will be so right for progression that a feeling of legato is produced even when there is no key connection.

"Staccato"—detachment—also assumes a different role for the pianist because it is far less dramatic when it does not interrupt a tone held with emotional intensity. Thus, as often as not, a staccato mark indicates emphasis and not detachment for the pianist. The importance of "legato" and "staccato" lies in their relation to emotional expression. This can mean only one thing ever: an intensification of the long-line rhythm which deals with the phrases as a whole. "Legato" and "staccato" have specific values for the pianist in gaining a technique; but they also have specific pitfalls. Legato, in slow practice, easily breeds sluggishness. Staccato, on the other hand, especially when slow practice is needed, uses a precise delivery of power and thus furthers ultimate speed, while at the moment a slow tempo is in operation.

But a staccato which breeds an "up" action—an action for flying away from the keyboard—develops a habit which opposes top speed and rhythmic continuity. It can be most damaging to phrase modeling. All one needs for detachment is the cessation of the positive power which produced the tone. The key will come up if it is not held down. The shortest possible application of power is the formula for staccato—not a flying off the keyboard.

4 A Simple Statement of Activity in Torso and Arms. An Explanation of Terms Used in Relation to a Specific Action

All action involves bones and muscles. The bony structure—the resistive element—makes the action of muscles effective.

Muscles contract and relax—nothing more. They act in areas and not in the isolated manner of the strings which manipulate a marionette.

The torso functions in two ways, never unrelated for the pianist:

a. As a part of the fundamental rhythm.

b. As the fulcrum for the full arm.

The arm is connected with the torso by a circular joint which allows the arm full play in all directions.

The forearm as a whole acts through a hinge joint at the

elbow by flexion and extension in one plane. It possesses two bones which twist and untwist to produce a rotary action.

The hand operates through the complicated wrist joint and can move with limitations in all directions. The up and down actions play through a wider arc of distance than actions from side to side.

The fingers move through three joints, two of them hinge joints with actions of flexion and extension only. The hand knuckle joint allows a limited rotation as well as flexion and extension. It is action at this third joint, the center of the radius of activity for the finger, with which the pianist is involved.

The thumb is the master mechanic of the hand. At its third joint—the wrist joint—it moves in all directions with easy freedom.

AN EXPLANATION OF TERMS USED IN RELATION
TO A SPECIFIC ACTION

Since there is no established vocabulary among teachers, as there is no uniformity in their teaching, each teacher uses words and phrases in relation to specific actions to save undue talking and to help clarify statements. Mine follow:

1. *Rhythm*—I feel strongly that rhythm should never be used for meter and note values (although they are a part of the larger rhythm), but should be reserved for that continuous undulating action which, once started, is impelled to carry the entire musical performance to its close.

2. *Meter* is used to mean time values of notes as opposed to the time value of musical ideas, to which the physical rhythm is attached.

3. *Rocking in a rhythm*—using an exaggerated movement of the torso from side to side for producing a tone. This is one manner of connecting up the action of the torso with a musical pattern.

4. *Emotional rhythm*—the combination is good imagery for suggesting one of the pianist's greatest assets: a basic rhythm

which is the outlet for the emotional reaction to the music. It is like the thrill of skating or dancing.

5. *Line*—A line in performance means playing which spins an unbroken thread through the relationship of parts. It is the antithesis of playing which breaks with bar lines and ends of phrases. This line is the product of the manner in which rhythmic nuances and dynamics are handled.

6. *Destination* is made to incorporate the physical action which is never interrupted by the movements of articulation as it heads for its goal. It is simple to understand that a phrase is a grouping of tones—harmonically, melodically and metrically—which makes an intelligible musical statement. That grouping consumes time in playing. Destination is used to mean the continuous physical action which measures out that span of time. It starts and never stops until the goal is reached. A glissando is a good illustration of such a movement.

7. *Pulsing*—pulsing, outlining or scanning the music indicates a reading which leaves out everything which can be deleted without destroying the emotional reaction to the beauty of the music. It is something like the relation of a telegram to a complete statement which includes all the modifiers—but with one signal difference: the telegram loses the grace of the full sentence, whereas pulsing is used to intensify the awareness of the grace in relationship of the important tones of the music. A basic rhythm uses these important tones as stepping stones, as it were, in the music. Pulsing is a way of increasing the importance of the relationship of these stepping stones and of using them to enhance the grace in musical procedure (see page 145).

8. *Physical form*—used to stress the actual physical activity which is the counterpart of the musical form. It always intends to indicate that if one would clarify the musical form (the structural skeleton of the music), there must be a physical action which is related to and outlines that form. This is just another means of intensifying the necessity for a fundamental rhythm.

9. *Smallest musical unit*—a phrase to alert the pupil to a procedure by form, as opposed to a procedure by meter. This unit, in general, has as its minimum two measures.

10. *Fulcrum*—"Point against which lever is placed to get purchase or on which it turns or is supported." (*Oxford Dictionary*) The torso acts as fulcrum for the full arm. Top arm acts as fulcrum for movements involved in fast articulation of the forearm.

11. *Articulation*—"Hence by a slight extension articulation may also mean to make the manipulation or articulation for the sounds as a whole in one's speech." (*Webster*) Used for the piano as the manipulation of the key-drop: the vertical action which contacts tone.

12. *The center of the radius of activity*—For the full arm (the playing mechanism), it is the shoulder joint. For the movements of fast articulation, it is the elbow joint. For the finger, it is the hand knuckle joint; for the thumb, the wrist joint.

13. *Pull*—the word is accurate to connote the manner in which the energy of the top arm is applied to the key. It is also a word full of good imagery for the application of power to our percussive instrument, for "pull" helps to avoid a bearing-down action with the shoulder girdle. All energy applied by the top arm is delivered through movement which describes an arc of a circle. Because the playing stance places the point of the elbow slightly in front of the torso (the arm being slightly lifted), the only action which could put the key down, with the top arm, is a lowering of the arm. This lowering is actually a *pulling* of the arm toward the torso. The word "pull" also includes the shortening from shoulder to fingertip—that is actually the strongest sensation of "pull." This shortening, however, in no way prevents the ability of the humerus in the shoulder joint to turn in any direction. When the top arm takes key-drop, which it should always do when the mechanism is in contact

with the keyboard, the direction of the activity in the top arm is a "pull" toward the body.

14. *Level*—used to indicate the spot in the key-drop when the hammer trips and hits the string. It becomes excellent imagery for the releasing of power for tone instantly as the keybed is reached.

15. *Focus*—applied to energy. To focus the energy, use it only when it can be productive of tone. Use it with precision at the *level* for tone.

16. *Staying down*—Some part of the mechanism should control the level consistently for fast efficient playing. It should be the top arm. "Staying down" is consciously related to the pull of the top arm. It is the natural relation of top arm to hand in playing a glissando. It is the action which makes the top arm a fulcrum for fast articulation with the forearm.

17. *Horizontal progression*—needs no explanation as it stands. However, because it vividly opposes the vertical key action, it is related to the physical action of continuity—the counterpart of form—as opposed to the action for hitting single tones. In this relation it is often a suspended action, an intense feeling of the progress of the music even though there may be no actual progression along the keyboard.

18. *Traveling*—a purely suggestive term for a specific relationship between the movements of articulation and power. The torso and top arm are the main fulcrums. It is the top arm plus the torso, the central force, which motivates the over-all rhythm. Unless the movements for articulation are inside the orbit of this rhythm—timed with it—no fundamental rhythm can be effective in phrase modeling. Traveling, "going out on their own," is used to indicate that the actions of articulation are used independently of the top-arm rhythm. This rhythmic action actually furnishes a part of the power which is tone producing—a glissando illustrates this action by the fundamental power. Another illustration of this relationship is afforded by a fast violent sounding of five consecutive tones—"ripping" five

keys—when one is only conscious of the one strong action in the top arm. This action delivers power at the keybed. The power (meaning the upper arm action) moves directly into the tone (key-drop)—and through it, as it were. Traveling means that this contributing power for tone by the top arm is absent and only the action taking key-drop has produced the tone. This is another way of pointing out impediments placed in the way of an embracing rhythm.

19. *Direction*—"Your direction is faulty" is a very frequent diagnosis for trouble in a difficult passage. The central control of horizontal distance on the keyboard is linked with the long line of ascent or descent. A slight jog in the opposite direction must be taken with short levers without changing the *direction* of the control of the top arm, which is the central control for horizontal distance.

20. *Outside the power stream*—has no meaning whatsoever if one believes in the separate initiation of power for each single tone by the fingers. It is used to indicate that just that thing is happening: the fingers are not being coordinated with a central power. A fundamental rhythm is only operative in influencing the use of dynamics when fingers are a synchronized part of the operation of the total arm.

21. *Against bone*—an awareness of the arm as one bone when force is applied at the key is a manner of sensing the use of a central power. Paying attention to a localized muscle action can easily cause trouble. "Not against bone" means there is no central power getting through in tone production, but that small levers have taken over and small muscles are being unduly burdened. Small muscles are *producing* tone instead of simply *lining up a bone* for the large muscles to play against.

22. *Alternating action*—that marvelous combination of flexion and extension between forearm and hand whereby the one can come up at the same time the other is going down.

23. *Throw. Drop. Snap.*—These are terms used for the movement of the hand when it has been produced by a quick action

of the forearm. The crack of the whip or the control of a lariat illustrates the control at center which produces action at the periphery. The *throw* indicates the movement of the hand when a quick vigorous flexion of the forearm drops the hand downward. The *snap* is a violent kind of action, such as is used in snapping the dust out of a small rug or the water out of a cloth. The value of these words lies in their illustrating the free play which can be achieved at the wrist joint when there is a strong action by the large muscles acting through the shoulder and elbow joints, while at the same time fingers and thumb are in effective use.

24. *Tucked in*—Certain tones, like the small modifiers in speech, must be "tucked in" on the way to important tones. This means they are played without emphasis. But the point is that in piano playing there must be a variety in the use of levers if these results are to be easily achieved: small levers take key-drop during the process of repeated action by a larger lever. This principle is at the very core of efficient and beautiful playing.

25. *Repeated action*—discussed later in detail. The term is used to emphasize that a repeated action includes a down and an up action, and that the up action can be related to tone production by a combination of actions by other levers.

5   Techniques Other than with Fingers

Here is a diamond mine for the pianist. Once it is explored and put in operation, all the native resources are so utilized that the playing of the artist no longer seems remote, incredible and impossible. For there is no superlative playing which does not use to the full all the possibilities of the playing mechanism.

The training of performers is lopsided when it falls short of utilizing all the possibilities for a blended action in playing. The myriad infinitesimal differences in the balance and play throughout the body which are used for these "other techniques" can only be suggested. The combinations are too subtle and varied for factual analysis. In trying to pin words to these movements, a clumsiness is felt which never exists in actual performance.

Certain of these techniques need less training than others because they are inevitably brought into action by the performer's relation to the keyboard. The distance of the keyboard could not be covered, nor the hand be placed in playing position, without the combination of the turning of the top arm with the flexion and extension of the forearm, as well as the twisting of the two bones in the forearm (rotary action). These are actions which are automatically blended and used naturally, unless teaching superimposes a strait jacket.

Teaching should keep these movements in balanced activity, but there is no actual learning of their combinations. They are already learned and ready for adaptation to the pianist's needs. The activity involved in these "other techniques" has been unheeded because of the emphasis generally placed on the finger technique. It should have greater attention than fingers because it creates the rhythm and implements it, and because fingers are only the periphery of the total activity involved in playing. The action at periphery cannot promote the blended coordination demanded for virtuosity.

The other techniques belong to:

a. Torso. In a sitting position the resistance which makes the delivery of power effective is the chair seat. The torso rests upon a chair seat against the two ischial bones of the pelvis. For the pianist the muscles under these ischial bones create activity in the torso, much as manipulation of the feet against the floor resistance creates activity in the entire body as we stand. It is easy to feel the rhythm of skating and dancing when movement is not restricted. It is less easy to feel the same rhythmic exhilaration when the sitting posture limits movement. But it is exactly the same rhythmic response to the music which is so natural in dancing and skating that is needed for a thrilling performance at the piano—a response throughout the body.

We sit upon a cushion of large muscles. By contracting these muscles the cushion becomes thicker and harder, and the torso is boosted slightly higher. By relaxing these same muscles the cushion becomes thinner and softer, and the torso is lowered: the bones are closer to the chair seat.

This contraction and relaxation can be sudden or it may be gradual. When it is sudden, the effect is a sort of bouncing up and down of the torso; the torso dances the *gigue*. When the muscular action is gradual, one contraction may last for a long crescendo, and the relaxation may be sustained for the following decrescendo; the torso dances a slow waltz. This activity, dancing, *is* the rhythm of the music for the pianist. These movements are an extension of the action of the top arm—a necessary part of the total mechanism for articulating tone.

Besides these important lifting and lowering actions, this cushion of muscles can sway the torso in all directions, and in so doing create an outlet for the rhythmic response to the music.

To annihilate this activity of the torso by labeling it mannerism and objectionable is to dam up a source of emotional expression without which a performance loses its reason for being. Either the emotional expression is inhibited or it finds its outlet in the movements of articulation. One thing or the other is almost as damaging to the performance—insufficient expression or far too many explosions and climaxes.

The physical expression of the *emotion* of a dramatic sforzando or pianissimo may be, as a part of the delivery of power, a sudden relaxing of the spine, a collapse in the middle of the torso. Not uncommonly one sees a lifting of the entire torso away from the chair seat. This involves a transfer of resistance to feet and floor, away from ischial bones and chair seat. It is not unlike the transfer from saddle to stirrup in posting.

Any or all of these movements may constitute the activity which expresses the rhythmic and emotional response to the music in conjunction with the delivery of power. The cultivation of these movements will heighten the awareness of the relation of a fundamental rhythm to the production of subtle phrase modeling. The activity of the torso as a fulcrum for the articulating of tone is creative rhythmically—because it is absolutely a part of the activity of the top arm. "Sit in the driver's seat and hold the reins" is good imagery for fulcrum activity. Being well seated in the driver's seat is the only way to implement the holding of the reins. But it does not mean a stodgy sitting—rather, an alive, active part of the whole performance.

b. Top arm. The top arm motivates the full arm action and acts as a fulcrum for fast articulation by the forearm.

First of all it is the center of the radius of activity of the mechanism which gauges distance and delivers power to the key. Because it operates through a circular joint it possesses that unqualified blessing for the pianist: continuity in action. By means of this continuity in action, it produces the movement which initiates the fundamental phrase-wise rhythm—the counterpart of the musical idea. It does this by actually controlling key-drop and tone for important musical tones, and, in between these musical stepping stones, acting as a fulcrum for the forearm.

The top arm becomes the arbiter of spacing with these two capacities. It "holds the reins" for all fast articulation of tone.

It operates in all its functioning in relation to tone production through a pull, or draw. Only when this pull of the top arm is actively involved in sharing the production of all tones can full speed and power be achieved without the overburdening of small muscles. Such overburdening easily and frequently produces a crippling strain as well as inadequate facility.

It is when the top arm is consistently alerted to tone production that playing looks so astonishingly easy. By its response to the aural image, the rhythm of the *phrase* can become fused with the aural image—the end and aim of all playing habits. It can achieve this balance because as it strides from one important tone of the phrase to another, it produces an activity which is continuous and which outlines the phrase as a whole.

If one is to listen to the phrase as a whole there must be an activity which emphasizes direct progression from the first to the

last tone of the phrase and is a part of the power for tone production.

To establish a definite consciousness of this top arm activity,
it is valuable to have a practice tool which is its special instigator. The following skipping octave pattern is suggested for
that purpose:

Ill. 1

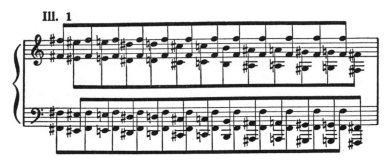

Only a very moderate tempo can be used without bringing
into play other levers—so keep it slow. Listen only to the chromatic scale: that is, consider the chromatic scale the all-important musical idea—the phrase. The repeated tone gets played
with a minimum of attention.

Use both arms but attend to the playing of only one arm,
while the other maintains a fixed distance and seemingly operates in conjunction with its partner. Use the pattern with the
scale going up or down.

This is not a complicated pattern but it may take days, weeks
or months to achieve actual tone production, key-drop control,
with action in the top arm only.

Away from the keyboard it is a simple matter to instigate this
control. But at the keyboard, if there are established habits of
controlling distance and tone with fingers, all the muscles governing the hand will fairly leap into action the moment tone is
approached.

The reward of possessing a direct control of tone with the top
arm is worth any time it takes to achieve it. By its possession,

playing can be enormously simplified. Without it, there is no chance of ever feeling that playing is really simple in its mechanics. With it, there is a center to periphery control: this produces simplicity in coordination. Without it, periphery takes over because the hand (the periphery) contacts the key. This produces every complication in production.

The octave pattern for establishing a top arm control of key-drop has various by-products of pertinent value:

1. The control of the *level* at which the energy for tone is released is maintained at the center of the playing mechanism. It must be there if control of the vertical distance is a blended control and not given over to a control uncoordinated with the central power. This awareness of a level (for all practical purposes the keybed) at which energy is released is the governing factor in having a precision in the use of energy. Either energy is used with conservation because it is made effective at the place where it is productive of tone, or it is wasted by being diffused over an area of distance in which it is not contacting tone production. A focused energy is always a part of great playing. When the top arm gauges this level everything has a chance to be "under control." When this level is not gauged from the center, everything can be out from under a central control and working without supplementary assistance.

2. The feeling that the arm is one bone from shoulder to tip of finger—the refinement of the sensation of a bony structure used as a unit—can be made the tool with which to check on perfect timing for the blended activity of all the levers sharing production of tone.

This unified bony structure exists when the top arm is actually in control of key-drop and tone. When the right level for using power is established—no pressure against keybed after tone is produced, no sticking—there is a synchronization of controls of distance, power and level. At one special split second, these factors operate together. There is no such special split second in the production of tone when perfect timing is not present. If the feeling of *one bone* comes into existence at all it will be after tone has been produced. It will come with pressure against keybed—a pressure which uses energy with complete ineffectiveness so far as tone production is concerned. No top speed with brilliance is possible with wasted energy.

Timing is a prerequisite for any world's record in sports. Piano playing is as exacting as any sport for a top flight performance. A simple tool which can highlight this element of timing is of enormous value. Awareness of the bony structure as a unit at the second of tone production can develop into such a tool. The skipping octave pattern can be used to establish this awareness of bony structure.

3. The full arm stroke furnishes a mechanism for playing upon an initial reading (learning the notes) which does the least possible damage to a going rhythm. If one is a poor sight reader and without keen pitch perception, a slow tempo is necessary in making contact with new music, regardless of the fact that it may be very undesirable for the tempo of a final performance. Because there can be continuity in action when using the full arm stroke, it does less damage in a note-wise procedure than using only a part of the mechanism, such as fingers, when reading.

Observe that the octave pattern will not be a note-wise procedure if the ear attends only to the chromatic scale. The repeated tone is played without diverting the ear away from the sequence of the tones that make up the scale. Observe also that listening with the attention on the scale will make a difference both in the ease with which accuracy is achieved and the heightening of the beauty of the scale as a musical phrase.

Use this pattern as a command performance for avoiding stopping because of inaccuracy. There is no valid reason ever for stopping in the middle of a phrase except for the loss of the pitch image of the tones which are to follow.

Use every possible chance, which means ALL PRACTICE AT ALL TIMES, for furthering rhythmic completion in action as the counterpart of the aural image of the musical idea. This octave pattern can serve efficiently in this regard.

The *top arm* used as a fulcrum can only be fully understood when once there is a most sensitive awareness of action which takes place through the shoulder joint. Action does not necessarily mean the moving of a lever; it may mean simply holding that lever in alert readiness for movement. It certainly does not mean relaxation. It is the cat ready to spring—not the cat sleeping in the sun.

The top arm as fulcrum has found the level at which tone is produced and remains alerted to maintain that level, while the short levers, by releasing the key and taking key-drop, disconnect and connect up with its current of activity for producing tone. Not only is the top arm alerted for standing at attention for momentarily produced power, but it is alerted for a resistance to the action of small levers—is a fulcrum for that action. The pull of the top arm producing movement which goes into production of tone at key level must be sufficiently active not to slip out of its stance when the short levers act against it. This pull can be activated by an infinitesimal turning of the humerus.

Depending on tempo and speed of sequence of tones, one stance of the top arm may serve as the fulcrum for many articulations by short levers. Then it will take over the production of another important tone and, in so doing, assume another stance. As it acts in this capacity of fulcrum, it controls the spacing between tones: it actively holds the reins of the actions by small levers.

The pianist's phrase modeling is dependent upon the kind of activity which takes place between tones. Is that space filled in with the movements of articulation? If so, the fundamental rhythm cannot be actively involved. Is it, on the other hand, filled in by action in top arm and torso? If so, the fundamental rhythm takes on greater and greater importance in relation to tone production.

Habits of action must all further a rhythm if playing is to develop constantly in musical perception.

Use imagery for gaining a technique in the top arm. We consistently use the total arm as one lever in our daily activities, such as pulling down a window sash, turning the steering wheel of a car, hoeing in the garden, sweeping, etc. In all these activities the forearm and hand extend the action of the top arm; they make the top arm action effective. But it is the action in the top arm which furnishes the positive movement for these activities, and this movement is the natural coordinator of all the activity in forearm and hand which implements its efficiency.

We need just such a fundamental coordinator for piano playing. Here are two means for achieving this desired control by the top arm:

Ill. 2

Fold up the forearm and pantomime the pattern with the top arm. Hum the chromatic scale if it helps to center attention on the scale. When the top arm easily moves as if to produce tone in response to the aural image, gradually assume the playing stance with forearm and hand. Do this without interruption of the aural image of the scale and the accompanying action of the top arm. About halfway down the scale let actual tone production take place without the hand's assuming control. The hand must simply extend the control of the top arm.

Or play F♯ and remain there holding the key down. While holding, take pains to register whether the down action is a control of the top arm, or a down *pressure* in the forearm and hand which is actively usurping the holding down of the key. In sensing this relationship of top arm to forearm, think of the top arm as tipped down, while the forearm and hand are tipped up and feel light. Then gently but definitely setting this relationship between top arm and forearm and hand, move the top arm forward until the hand swings free of the keyboard (total movement made only at the shoulder joint). Then use the reverse of this action—swing the top arm downward toward the torso, until the hand contacts keybed again (not with any volition on the part of the forearm and hand but because they are simply the extension of the top arm).

Think in terms of a three-section telescope while operating this action. Shove the hand into the forearm, forearm into top arm, so that only one section remains for movement.

With persistence, the top arm will become astute in using the controls which rightfully belong to it for expertness in making music at the piano.

c. Forearm. The *alternating action* (that combination between forearm and hand which allows the dream of speed without torture to come true) plus the rotary action are the truly master mechanics for speed with brilliance in piano playing. If the alternating action received anything like the attention in learning which fingers have been given, there would be a great increase in facility for those players who are now endowed with what seems like a ready-made coordination. All who are thus richly endowed use the alternating action whether they know it or not.

The combination of leverage between elbow and wrist which produces the alternating action avoids a vacant up action—vacant of tone production—which means speed in tone production with half the speed in a repeated action. (It is like the trill of the violinist: while the finger is lifted the string is producing tone.) While the forearm lifts, the hand goes down. The hand produces tone while the forearm gets ready to repeat a down action. All that is necessary for a tone is a down action at some point. If there is no vacuum so far as tone production is concerned while an up action is taking place, that horrible feeling of jamming and being unable to achieve speed is relieved.

The alternating action turns that comforting trick. It operates in two ways: one when there is positive control at the wrist of the hand action, and the other when the muscles governing the hand are passive and the action of the forearm flings the hand down or out.

It is this possibility of flinging the hand down or out through the wrist joint which gives the wrist a very specialized value for the pianist. It means, as with the crack of the whip, that power used through a very small arc can produce the movement which will cover a much wider arc of distance. Thus, a quick small movement at the elbow can fling the hand in such a manner that it will cover distance—horizontal, vertical, and in-and-out—expertly. This is great conservation in movement.

A prime necessity of speed and brilliance is a compactness in the use of power for control of distance as well as for tone. There has been much discussion concerning a "loose wrist." The wrist is only effectively "loose" when it allows an action farther back in the arm to propel the hand through an arc of distance. Then its "looseness" is of the utmost importance.

The determining factors as to whether the muscles governing the hand are active or passive as the hand takes distance are the matter of the arc of distance and whether one tone only is produced with a down action of the hand or forearm, or whether one down action of forearm or hand must cover the articulation of two or more tones.

Ill. 3

Illustration 3 (Chopin, Etude, Op. 10, No. 7) uses a drop of the hand for the thirds and a "thrown" hand for the sixths. The thirds are always the trouble makers in this Etude because the down action needed for articulation must be taken with hand or fingers. If the fingers take over, it is hopelessly fatiguing. If the hand takes over too soon, it is still too tiring for any real virtuosity in playing the Etude. A quick flexion at elbow must throw the hand down, and the top arm staying down as fulcrum acts with the pull sufficiently to relieve the hand of any vitalization except at the last split second.

The down action of the forearm throws the hand out for the position of placing the sixth as the down action of forearm takes the key-drop. The hand becomes simply the extension of that down action.

Ill. 4

Illustration 4 (Chopin, Etude, Op. 25, No. 9) is a pattern showing one flexion of forearm covering two articulations by the hand (two middle 16ths) and one extension of forearm is divided between the fourth and the first 16ths of the group.

Illustration 5 (Chopin, Prelude, Op. 28, No. 8) aptly shows alternating action as related to finger action. Here the hand is not dropped or thrown by action of the forearm, but has movement controlled through the wrist. Extension of the forearm is

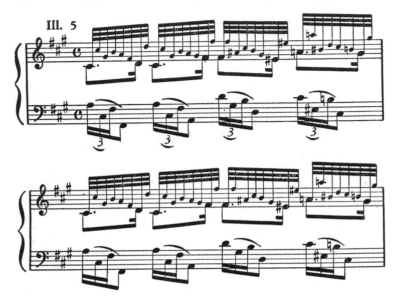

Ill. 5

used with the thumb, and one flexion of the forearm covers the fingers used between thumb actions.

Rotary action. Rotary action is well known as an incomparable asset in playing. Its combination with the alternating action makes the technique of the forearm loom large in any facility which qualifies as virtuosity.

Passing. Here we are faced with a welter of stress in traditional teaching concerning the exact movements that should take place with finger and thumbs.

If I could blast these concepts right out of existence I would not hesitate to do so. That is how faulty and pernicious I think they are. They can literally cripple a pianist if they are put into actual operation. Virtuosity demands that this technique of passing the hand along the keyboard be a blended activity involving every possibility from shoulder to fingers. Certainly that can only mean that the action is initiated at the center of the radius of activity and not at periphery. Thumb and fingers follow through with perfect timing, but they do not and should not initiate the control for either distance or power. When a movement is necessitated for the completion of an act, nature will supply one which is right in proportion.

An excellent test for faulty or correct passing is to check on one's reaction to a swift and beautiful scale or arpeggio when listening to a virtuoso performance. Do you wonder how on earth the pianist can play so fast and hit all the keys with accuracy? Or do you have a consuming desire to get to your piano and try to produce a scale which is equally beautiful? Does it seem impossible—or possible, given a little time?

If it seems quite hopelessly impossible and you have no glimmer of an idea as to how it can be accomplished, then you are trying with a coordination which actually makes a scale an impossible feat. It means thumb snapping under the palm and reaching for position; and fingers trying to reach over the thumb and seeking a legato key connection. It doesn't matter if the performer achieving the swift and beautiful scales and arpeggios tells you he does just that—it isn't true. No suggestion is meant that he is lying, but simply that he was successful in discarding the coordination that he was taught when the occasion arose which made it inadequate. He may well have made the transition unconsciously. Or more than likely he never actually made the exact actions which were indicated in the teaching. His gift was great enough to clear the tracks when speed demanded that they be free of obstructions.

The tragic thing is that a large percentage, even among talented people, cannot clear the tracks of faulty habits in that manner. They have to be re-educated physically to a new pattern of coordination; and that re-education can mean a period of wretched misery to them. They lose their fun in playing during the process.

Take away thumb and fingers, and what is left for passing? You will be surprised how little the fingers need to do when all the "other techniques" take responsibility for passing and legato key connection is not adhered to.

Action can be taken through the shoulder joint in any direction. The top arm can move so that the elbow end of the humerus can describe a segment of a circle, up or down, in and out, back and forth, or around and about. By this easy turning process of the head of the humerus in the shoulder joint, the hinge joint at the elbow is made easily adaptable for using the forearm in any plane. Quick flexion or extension plus the rotary action of the forearm can throw the hand down or out or sidewise, and by so doing create a relationship in action between the elbow and the wrist: the handle and tip of the whip. A tiny movement of the handle can produce a wider movement at the tip. This relationship is most valuable for an arpeggio with wide chord formation. These same movements of the hand can of course be controlled at the wrist.

This flexion or extension of forearm plus rotary action, plus the constant easy adjustment at the shoulder, can put the hand in successive playing positions along the keyboard. As a matter of fact, even when the thumb and fingers are made the chief agents of passing, these "other techniques" are present. The relationship, however, is almost reversed. The "other techniques" are, in a sense, dragged into the picture when thumb and fingers are trying to make the adjustment; when the "other techniques" are the positive control for placing the hand in position, the thumb and finger actions become simply an extension of the "other techniques"—a follow-through. Ease is always the result of a coordination from center to periphery. With control from center the entire coordination operates to make it easy to have a finger available at the moment it is needed for transmitting the power of the arm.

The best proof of this statement is a beautiful scale or arpeggio played with complete disregard for any conventional fingering. This often happens with a gifted, untaught pianist. There simply seems to be no difficulty in having a finger ready to transmit power. The entire mechanism is serving the needs of swift change in the position of the hand along the keyboard.

Every teacher with a gifted child has had the experience of seeing the child play a fast passage with what seems a crazy fingering. But he plays the passage with fluency and with no thought of its being difficult. Every possible adjustment has come to his aid, and one finger over another has been just as convenient as a so-called properly passed thumb.

All technical problems of distance—and surely passing is one of these—if solved easily, bring into play *all* the movements which can be useful. They are not solved by using *one* movement in exaggeration. No one action is adequate—even the action at the center of the radius of activity. But only that action can coordinate all the levers needed.

For passing, the top arm acts as a fulcrum for all the "other techniques" involving the forearm and hand: flexion and extension at elbow, rotary action, and lateral hand action at wrist, and last and least, lateral action of fingers and thumb.

After horizontal distance is accounted for, there is the vertical action of the key to be taken care of. Again let the finger and thumb action be a follow-through, a coordinated movement with alternating action and rotary. The alternating action is a must for easy passing. It needs more attention than rotary action for the simple reason that no playing can take place without the rotary action. Rotary is unavoidably and naturally on tap; this is not true of the alternating action. Its superlative assistance and functioning are allowed to go unheralded. Traditional concepts do not make much of it. But there it is, ready to take over in a marvelously expert manner and to relieve the fingers and thumb of initiating the action for taking key-drop in passing.

Between rotary action and alternating action, passing is made as easy as it looks when the expert does it.

6 Some Questions and Answers Dealing with Traditional Teaching Methods

1. *Should the hand be trained for action independent of the arm?*
2. *Should the fingers be trained to find the key—to reach for position?*
3. *Should fingers be trained to produce the power for tone which involves trying to make them equal in hitting strength?*
4. *Should fingering be stressed?*
5. *Is hand position a creative factor in developing a technique?*
6. *Should Hanon and Czerny have high rating as material to be used?*

7. Are scales desirable at an early stage as a means for developing fluency?
8. Does "preparation" solve or create a problem?
9. Is "touch" a fallacy for the pianist?
10. Are various kinds of movements necessary for playing staccato?
11. Is legato playing the same kind of asset musically with the piano as it is with the instruments which produce tone by breath or bow?
12. Are octaves played from the wrist?
13. How important is it to train the rotary action as an individualized action?
14. Is relaxation the basis of easy speed?
15. Can weight—an inert pressure—help develop facility?
16. Is slow practice always a virtue? Does slow practice further accuracy in a fast tempo?
17. What is the relation of routine drill to the action which furthers an exciting rhythm?
18. Are rests an interruption of rhythmic continuity?
19. Does counting develop a vivid awareness of time values?
20. What is the result of having details take precedence in the learning of a composition?
21. Are difficulties in rapid passage work solved by breaking up the large pattern into small units for detailed work?
22. How valuable are editors' marks in developing musical judgment and taste?
23. Can coaching solve the musical difficulties inherent, say, in playing a Beethoven Sonata?

1. Should the hand be trained for action independent of the arm?

No. For the very simple reason that any skilled coordination takes place from the center to periphery—not from periphery to center. The hand is the periphery of the playing mechanism. If it is trained to act independently, habits are established which definitely interfere with any balance of activity throughout the arm. Since the hand alone is not adequate for playing the piano, the habits of action it acquires should be the habits which make it a synchronized part of the entire mechanism. It demands just as much skill to fulfill this role of being an expert part of the whole, but it is a different role. It makes no sense to train the hand to act independently when virtuoso playing demands that it act as a part of the whole.

2. *Should the fingers be trained to find the key—to reach for position?*

Never! The key must be found before the tone can be produced. It is the first necessary action in playing. If it is faulty, everything else will have difficulty in being right. A sense of reaching for the key with the fingers tends to disengage their action from the arms and thus make all horizontal distance feel enormously wide. It is thinking and gauging distance at the center and not at the periphery (like the compass) which makes all horizontal distance at the keyboard easily negotiable. Only then can there be a blended action by all possible levers for taking that distance. Fingers should not be trained to, or allowed to, reach for key position. No easy control for horizontal distance can ever be achieved if such a habit sticks in the mechanics of performance.

3. *Should the fingers be trained to produce the power for tone, which involves trying to make them equal in hitting strength?*

What is the sense in establishing habits which do not conform to the greatest efficiency in using power? A habit is a habit; once it is formed it is there to hinder progress when it does not lend its skill to the total picture of playing. It is the worst possible use of time to establish habits which do not fit into the ultimate pattern of what is demanded for virtuosity. Fingers can never be made equal in hitting strength and they have insufficient power for a fortissimo. And what about a pianissimo? Are they the most expert control there? My answer is, watch what you do when achieving a delicate task which has no relation to piano playing. If you had to take a splinter out of a child's eye, would you do it with finger action unrelated to the coordination of the arm, or would you do it with an action which involved a coordination from head to toe? Of course you would instinctively be completely coordinated to insure gauging the movement with the greatest possible accuracy. I remember trying to get a dependable control for the last two chords of the Chopin Berceuse. Try as I might, I could never be sure that they would sound. Fingers were in control of the pianissimo. Not until I learned, years later, that no pianissimo can be certain unless there is a complete coordination of the arm, did I know why I could not be sure of those chords. If one can have no control for a pianissimo or fortissimo with fingers, why set up a habit for the in-betweens of gradation— a control which will balk the achieving of the extremes in dynamic variations? Extremes in dynamics are highly desirable; they are a part of all dramatic expression.

When the fingers can so easily furnish a bone for the large muscles to play against, why spend years developing power in the muscles governing the fingers? They will achieve what power is needed when they act as an integrated part of the power stream furnished by large muscles. Training the fingers for hitting strength is the basis for all "pianists' cramp"; and, worst of all, fingers trained to produce the power for tone set up a mechanism for an independent initiation of power. This means no fundamental rhythm is coordinating a technique for producing dynamics with ease and subtlety in control.

There is no argument for this procedure in training fingers to furnish the power for tone, except that it has always been done. Yet no top-notch performance is ever the result of this kind of use of power. It simply cannot be done. It takes the total coordination with a rhythm underneath to produce that kind of performance.

4. *Should fingering be stressed?*

I should say that the importance of a prescribed fingering is practically nil. If you avoid fussing about fingering you will never produce a lasting obstacle to fluent passage work. If a rhythm is working, a finger will be ready to deliver power.

5. *Is hand position a creative factor in developing a technique?*

No, because it is the periphery of the playing mechanism and creative factors all lie at the center of the radius of activity and inherently operate in coordination with a rhythm. There is too wide a variance in hand position with fluent players to give it a high priority among creative factors in developing facility.

6. *Should Hanon and Czerny have a high rating as material to be used?*

They should be completely discarded on the sole basis that they are not sufficiently stimulating musically to further music-making. There is no time to waste on dull literature, for the mechanism can be coordinated expertly only when there is excitement and intensity of desire for accomplishment in the practice period. "Practice" should never mean working without any of the fun that is attached to playing. Certainly Hanon and Czerny are no fun, and they deserve to be permanently shelved on that basis.

7. *Are scales desirable at an early stage in developing fluency?*

The great beauty of a scale as a musical pattern should not be dimmed for a beginner by making it dull—that is, using it without its musical value. That is reason one. Reason two is that the scale is full of subtle difficulties which cannot possibly be realized until the mechanism has been greatly refined. A beautiful scale is the result of a beautifully balanced use of power and distance, and it is in no way an efficient tool for achieving that blend in balanced activity. Any diatonic progression tends to emphasize the actions of articulation. A basic rhythm is more readily brought into play by large skips. Used early as a form of technique, the scale is entirely a matter of finger production. When that happens, there are ten separate controls to be attended to, and with parallel motion these controls operate in opposition to each other.

A third reason for not using scales in acquiring facility is that with an inordinate amount of practice a scale can be played very well with fingers, and thus it does not help in making the pupil aware that virtuoso playing demands a balanced activity throughout the body.

There is value in using a difficult pattern early, but only the kind of pattern which balks until a right balance in activity is established. Octaves and double thirds are examples of this kind of useful difficulty. They remain difficult and practically unplayable until they are produced in the easiest possible manner. Thus they are extremely valuable in establishing a technique. But a good finger scale is of no assistance, or practically none, in playing arpeggios and double notes—so the time spent on scales is not used to the best advantage. They should not be used, as they still are in most conservatories, as a criterion of progress in accomplishment. Educators in other fields have learned to start with the large movements first in establishing a desirable coordination.

8. *Does "preparation" solve or create a problem?*

By "preparation" is meant two actions: one, as one finger takes the key-drop, having the next finger to be used snap into a lifted position; and two, moving into position for the tone to be sounded before the time has arrived when it is desired. The first action is only methodically insisted upon when the fingers are being trained to produce the power for tone. That lifted position means that the finger is getting ready to produce tone— the antithesis of what is demanded for top virtuosity and beauty in playing. The second action is believed to be of value in establishing accuracy. Actually, in its application, it destroys all subtle timing. It damages a fundamental rhythm by emphasizing the actions of articulation. Anything which damages a fundamental rhythm does not enhance the chances for accuracy. The second action makes for a procedure by dots and dashes, rather than smooth continuity. Phrase modeling demands smooth continuity to the close of the phrase.

9. *Is "touch" a fallacy for the pianist?*

This matter of "touch" serves as an excellent example of how influenced and often befogged our thinking is by an emotional reaction to a situation. One might as well save one's breath as to discuss "touch" with a pianist who believes in "tone quality." He will also believe in "touch" and, facts to the contrary, he will keep his beliefs. Here is an example of the association of listening with physical habits and emotional output. One presses the keybed because of emotional feeling for the tone, and the listening becomes associated with the pressure— "touch." The tone has not been influenced by that pressure but the performer has expressed emotions with it, and thus he has been led to believe that the quality of the tone was changed by it. For the pianist, there is no such thing as "touch" influencing the quality of tone because he is not in contact with the strings. There are percussive noises with tone production but they are not the tone which is produced by the string.

10. *Are various kinds of movements necessary for playing staccato?*

Of course not. The tone is staccato if the key is not held down. Staccato is dependent only on the cessation of the tone-producing energy. That need not involve any lifting away from the keyboard of the hand, forearm or full arm—a release at the finger joint will turn the trick.

This question has been included because any teaching of a certain type of up action—getting off the keyboard—is fallacious. Because an up action can be uninhibited it easily becomes associated with an emotional explosion. It is when this sort of action does become the expression of emotional intensity that there is danger to the continuous flow of rhythm and to a discreet—or better—sensitive handling of dynamics.

11. *Is legato playing the same kind of asset musically with the piano as it is with the instruments which produce tone by breath or bow?*

Using "legato" to mean holding the key down until the next is depressed in order to keep tone continuous (which is the basis of its usage as applied to the piano), I believe that it has nothing like the musical value that legato has with reference to those instruments which produce tone with breath or bow. This has been discussed in Chapter 3.

12. *Are octaves played from the wrist?*

Here is a confusion caused by a traditional concept which does not coincide with a natural coordination. Traditional procedure drills one lever to increase muscle strength and endurance as well as control. Nature uses a blend in action of all possible levers in accomplishing an expert result, and thus distributes the burden and avoids strain. When top speed and brilliance are produced in an octave passage by an expert, watch the effort which is being put forth by the entire body: there is action every place. It just happens that the movement at the wrist is the most obvious. It is the crack of the whip.

If octaves are produced by an entirely localized control at the wrist, they never attain top rank for speed and brilliance.

13. *How important is it to train rotary action as an individualized action?*

The objection to the stress put upon rotary action is that if there were no stress at all, it would operate with efficient skill. Nothing less than believing that one should be able to balance a penny on the back of the hand while playing will inhibit its natural use.

Rotary action is not quite the cure-all that it is frequently rated to be, for the reason that it takes place in forearm, and if it is given too much responsibility the top arm will not be used to the extent that is necessary for real virtuosity.

14. *Is relaxation the basis of easy speed?*

Whenever there is an argument about relaxation, there is also an insistence on qualifying the meaning of the word. That is one reason the word itself is bad for suggesting anything but what it does mean. Webster's definition is, "To make lax or loose." There you have it. Can you win a quarter-mile dash by being lax or loose? Is a cat lax or loose when it is being chased up a tree by a dog? Relaxation in no way suggests the alert blended coordination that is the basis for speed; and it develops habits of releasing power between tones. Rather, beautiful playing is related to the absence of releases. They ruin both a rhythm and the subtle use of dynamics—and then what have you?

Speed is the result of an alert blended balance in activity—not of relaxation.

15. *Can weight—an inert pressure—help develop facility?*

It is exactly the inert pressure of weight which cannot be used for speed. Words are important in teaching. Words of action are needed to suggest the coordination for speed. Weight does not suggest the muscular activity which moves the weight of the arm. It does suggest an inert pressure.

16. *Is slow practice always a virtue? Does slow practice further accuracy in a fast tempo?*

a. By no means! Quite the reverse. Slow practice can establish habits which are completely unrelated to the coordination demanded for speed. Add legato playing to slow practice and the result will be that one is tied to a post rather than skimming the ground.

b. The matter of accuracy which has led to the belief in slow practice hints at concentration on precision, while speed hints at taking chances. The physical attributes related to these attitudes are quite dissimilar—and therein lies the answer. Taking time out to insure that a finger finds the right key (I say finger purposely, for the finger being responsible for accuracy is the worst kind of fallacy) is no basis for insuring accuracy in speed. Accuracy in speed is dependent, first of all, on an accurate aural image; second, on the smooth continuity of a basic rhythm; and third, most emphatically on the right control for horizontal distance. This right control must be at the center of the radius of activity of the playing mechanism and not at its peripheral extensions. Slow practice may very well not include any of these attributes.

Accuracy is a deep taproot in the minds of practically all teachers. Accuracy of the aural image should have first place, always, but second in rank in production comes an unbroken rhythmic progression. Only this rhythm can produce accuracy with speed.

17. *What is the relation of routine drill to the action which furthers an exciting rhythm?*

If only we could remember that practice perfects exactly the coordination that it uses and not something else, and therefore we must use those practiced habits when the demand for playing is something quite different, we would know instantly that dull routine drill does not produce the blended activity needed for an exciting rhythm. Tradition believes in routine drill and never counts the cost which is piled up against the chances for achieving a rhythm. What is the harm in practicing an exciting rhythm? Why not have fun for an hour at the piano? Just thinking that difference in approach makes the corners of the mouth turn up and gives the body a feeling of exhilaration. Music is such a delightful and precious possession! Never dull its beauty if you can help it.

18. *Are rests an interruption of rhythmic continuity?*

They certainly should not be. Rests should be as full of action toward the desired goal as the held tone should be. Probably that is a bad simile, for too many pianists unfortunately rest on held tones. Say, rather, as full of progression as is the body of the polo pony when its feet are off the earth, as we see it in a slow-motion picture.

19. *Does counting develop a vivid awareness of time values?*

There are several reasons why counting is inadequate for developing a subtle sense of timing. Counting takes care of the sequence of beats; and after thinking about this matter for some time, I cannot make any other positive statement concerning it. On the negative side: one, it doesn't connect up with the physical action of progression where rhythm is ensconced. It could, if a definite association were made with physical activity, but that is not the manner in which it is used, as I have observed it. Two, counting makes time units a matter of addition only. When this relationship is established, tones are related to what has gone before—that is, they have only the relationship backward and no relationship forward. That is certainly unsound for the projection of a musical idea.

Three, counting is not concerned, as it is first learned certainly, with the time unit of the measure. Thus it establishes no mold of which the beats are a part, a subdivision.

Four, counting is an extraneous factor to the operation of playing. The subtle sensing of time values lies in the physical action of progression, a timing which is related to a rhythm. Counting is inadequate for developing a subtle rhythm, and therefore a subtle timing. It is never more than a crutch in getting an awareness of rhythmic timing.

20. *What is the result of having details take precedence in the learning of a composition?*

First impressions have an excellent chance of survival. If the first impressions of learning a composition deal with details, there are too many chances that those details will never assume their only pertinent value—that of lending beauty to the structure as a whole.

I remember so well a debut I once attended. No fault could be found with any of the details of the phrasing, but there was no pleasure in listening to the music. There was none of the flow of musical ideas that makes for enjoyable and easy listening; there was only that meticulous attention to each individual motive as it came along. It was just another debut that had accuracy in detail but no broad conception of the musical canvas. The habits necessary to making the broad strokes had been made too late, if at all. The habits formed in dealing with the details had conditioned the pianist's listening and playing. Practice will always favor that sad result, if details are given precedence in forming the feeling for a composition.

21. *Are difficulties in rapid passage work solved by breaking up the large pattern into small units for detailed work?*

Cortot's edition of the Chopin Etudes will serve as an example of this manner of tackling difficulties. This kind of solution is practically useless because it does not indicate the source of the difficulty. Inaccuracy in hitting a sequence of tones is due to one or more of the fundamental attributes of faulty playing. Difficulties are always the result of an over-use of small muscles and an under-use of large muscles. A balance in activity must be established if difficulties are to disappear. Practicing with a faulty balance in activity does not improve matters.

22. *How valuable are editors' marks in developing musical judgment and taste?*

It would be an easy way out if editors' marks could be effective in developing musical judgment and taste. I have found no evidence that they influence either the listening or the rhythmic habits out of which musical judgment and taste emerge. The most conclusive evidence in this regard has been in listening to string quartets. They pay great attention to editing, I am told. They practice together hours at a time and they use the same score of course. Yet one member of the quartet can be counted on always to deliver a phrase of sensitive beauty while the others never succeed in duplicating that beauty. No, editors' marks remain unable to touch the inner springs of musical judgment and taste. It takes a rhythm to do that.

23. *Can coaching solve the musical difficulties inherent, say, in playing a Beethoven Sonata?*

Without a gracious and sensitive rhythm in the body no one can project the inner meaning and beauty of a Beethoven Sonata. This rhythm is the output of physical activity. Coaching deals with intellectual concepts and traditional usage, and reproduction through imitation. It does not deal with the physical aspects of playing. Unless the pupil possesses a technique which consciously or unconsciously has always utilized a basic rhythm, he will lack the means to implement the coaching. His faults in interpretation will remain no matter how much he has learned in intellectual concepts.

7   Imagery—Memorizing—Pedaling—Phrasing—Channeling of Emotion

There are few short cuts in working for perfection. Imagery is one of them.

Failure in achieving a result, when working with a planned procedure which includes many repetitions of the balky passage, can sometimes be turned into success by a flash of good imagery.

When all is said and done, we do not know so very much about what actually happens in the body to make beautiful playing a reality. Nature has far greater skill in action than teachers have in making an analysis of that creative activity. Imagery touches off that capacity which is inherent in a skilled coordination.

We are accustomed to acting upon a thought. All we need is a desire, an imaged result, and we move and act expertly to get the thing we desire. What we do in action as a means to the result, we are totally unaware of most of the time.

Imagery suggests a kind of result. Say, for instance, you are dealing with a hand that is flabby or a hand that is tense. Either condition will change instantly if it is suggested that a delicate flower be held in the palm in a manner which will not crush it.

The same imagery will not always work in correcting a result. Sometimes it takes a lot of fishing to pull out the right imagery for the right person at the right time. But one word is enough if it works. It will create a result which no amount of practice and analysis has produced.

In an attempt to analyze the mechanics of playing, we are reduced to using terms which are used for machinery. The terms are accurate and, in the case of machinery, the operation which one expects is fulfilled. Apply the same term to our body mechanics and it is largely imagery which makes it work. The relationship in action is imaged because we understand the mechanics involved in the piece of machinery.

The use of the word *fulcrum* has been of great assistance to me. For instance, the torso is a fulcrum for the entire arm; the torso and top arm are fulcrums for fast articulation. In a sense, that is not imagery at all—it is fact. But it is the imagery which carries over from the use of the word in the field of machinery which makes the fact vivid in the relationships in the body. There is a logical reason why imagery serves us better than an attempt at an explicit account of the action of levers. Muscles act in areas, and when imagery stimulates a coordination there is no boundary line for these areas. There is, instead, cooperation from all the areas. When good imagery suggests a result there are far more chances for nature to take over the coordination in a skilled manner than when a so-called factual analysis of leverage is made.

I have no illusions concerning the effectual shifting of habits because of having read a printed page. But of one thing I am quite sure: whatever definite results do take place will be based on the working of some imagery.

When imagery has worked its charm, that is the time when it will be possible for the intellectual concepts of action to assist in the learning. "Imagination is more powerful than knowledge," says Einstein.

MEMORIZING

Here we are dealing with established habits of learning if, as is the case with this entire discussion, we are dealing with the problems found in players. But the players are not too different from young beginners, except that they have had more time to fix their habits. The young beginner needs smaller doses at a time and more frequent and greater assistance with practically no discussion of technique. He has no established concepts. Nature only needs to be given a chance.

I can sum up all that I know in relation to memorizing as follows:

1. With sound, the medium in question, the aural image is the only reliable memory. One recognizes music by its sound and in no other way. It is that image of the sound, with accuracy as to pitch or excellent relative pitch, which gives security in memorizing. It is the aural learners who have security with music memory.

2. Muscular habits in production of tone will determine the habits of listening and thus have a very definite bearing on memorizing. Note-wise procedure (single initiations of power, as with a finger technique) will develop note-wise listening, and that will hamper facility and security in memorizing. Muscular habits which correspond to a continuous flowing rhythm are a constructive assistance to memorizing. They keep attention on the statement as a whole, and parts are assimilated because they contribute to the meaning of the whole statement.

No functioning is at its peak of expertness without a fundamental rhythm acting as the one coordination for action. But no kinesthetic memory, of itself, is completely reliable—and least of all the note-wise finger type. Miss one tone and the entire listening and playing continuity can be destroyed.

3. The visual memory also is unreliable. A photographic memory can be of real assistance, but not many people have one. Even this kind of expert visual memory, however, is not what makes for a musical memory. Sight does not deal with sound, and for that reason it is not the memory to be stressed.

4. Association of ideas—this, for the musician, very largely means harmonic analysis. It is very doubtful that harmonic analysis actually functions at the time that playing is taking place. It is more valuable in influencing the manner of interpretation than in memorizing, as I have observed in students. For music, the aural image and basic rhythm are the two most productive factors in memorizing.

Since most students do their work by themselves, rote learning is not practical. If it were, I should put it first as a means for developing the aural image. If the eyes have never been involved in the learning, if ears alone have guided the movements that find the tones on the keyboard, there is the valuable "first experience" lending its tenacious quality to the most expert tool of remembering.

Next to rote learning comes transposition, which is completely practical for the student to develop by himself. The goal is a transposition by ear. If that is not possible in the beginning (that is, after one hears the page by having played the music) then use the printed text. The ear is inevitably involved in transposition, no matter what other processes are active at the same time.

Use the three keys immediately above and below the original, in transposing. Use a different key each day, and after each transposition try the composition without notes in the original key. If the music is written in the key of D, use E♭, E, F, D♭, C, and B for transposition. And play in D between each transposition, without notes.

It is easier for most people to transpose to a tonality not far away from the original key. Using a variety of keys for transposition and playing in the original key between each two transpositions, fixes the kinesthetic patterns in relation to the original key, which is desirable. Transposition does take time but it is time spent constructively. It extends one's capacities. Little by little there is developed a greater security, a greater sense of the sound of the keyboard. The ears learn to guide the movements to the key—which will produce the desired sound.

Nervousness in playing may be caused by a number of things, but certainly the fear of forgetting contributes to a great extent to that nervousness. When this is true, nothing but greater security in the aural memory can dissipate that nervousness. Transposition is the best means which I have found to be both practical and productive of the desired results.

PEDALING

Too much has been written on the subject of pedaling to make any long discussion here profitable. Also, good editing has been done in this field. There are a few main issues to keep well in mind:

Never allow the use of the damper pedal to become an outlet for rhythmic expression. That is, do not let movements of the foot, in relation to pedal, become a channel for feeling the meter. Excellent musicians frequently tap a meter with the foot, but that tap is not in connection with the damper pedal. Work without the damper pedal until there is a habitual expression of spacing and rhythm in the fulcrums of the playing mechanism.

The better the playing, the less the damper pedal is used. It should never be allowed to blur the etched outline of musical progression.

The soft pedal should be used more as a violinist uses a mute than for producing a soft tone. It can be most effective in producing a subdued passage, followed by a sparkling passage when it is released. It is of very little value for merely playing more softly.

The sustaining pedal is effective in holding musical organ points, and is often indicated by the composer when it is desired.

PHRASING

If phrasing could somehow assume an integrity of its own— that is, something besides a certain kind of reaction to editors' marks—then it could be a powerful ally of beautiful playing. At least in the teaching of phrasing, a superficiality that never significantly stimulates the right musical reaction is all too often the result attained.

The editing of phrasing more often stands in the way of finding the inner meaning of the music than it helps. That is the case, of course, because there is no physical counterpart of that phrase—no movement that is continuous and intensifies its meaning.

What is good phrasing? Is it not simply a clarification of the musical ideas? How does one learn to become acutely aware of phrase modeling?

I am sure that nothing is adequate for answering these questions except a greater and greater sensitivity to a long-line rhythm. When such a rhythm possesses and expresses the performer's reaction to the music, he can hardly fail to put forth phrases of grace and charm. When such a rhythm is absent from a performer's equipment, there can never be graceful phrase modeling.

No cognizance of phrase marks can tap the roots of illuminating playing. It takes an emotional rhythm to do that.

Thus, I would like to have phrasing mean, first of all, an absorbing rhythm; and, after that, the handling of the details of phrasing to augment that rhythm and not to destroy it.

CHANNELING OF EMOTION

The manner in which a performer expresses the force of the emotional response to the music he is playing can, and all too often does, determine the kind of performance which can be expected from him. The channeling of this emotion so that it creates beauty, but never distortion, in a phrase line poses a problem in teaching which every teacher would like to avoid.

The action, whatever it is, which expresses the intensity of feeling is an unconscious part of the projection of the music. We call these actions mannerisms, and often there is strenuous objection to them on the part of the audience.

There is only one sound basis for objecting to mannerisms: do they cause distortion of the phrase line? Unfortunately this is not the basis on which the objection is generally made. It is simply that they interfere with the pleasure of watching the performer.

But music is sound. It is hearing—not seeing—that should determine the beauty of a musical performance. We have no right, really, to criticize on any other basis.

In this aspect of performance the piano offers more pitfalls than the instruments which produce tone by breath or bow. Actually, the very fact that the key receives the power for tone makes it easy indeed to allow the emotional surge—the "mannerisms"—to become completely associated with the hitting process. Think well what that means for piano playing. It means that the pianist gets rid of his emotions, in far too great a measure, by increasing the intensity of hitting. That is, the more excitement, the louder the playing, and this loudness almost necessarily will be associated with individual tones or chords. There is insufficient capacity, even in moderately fast playing, for successive tones to be loud enough to satisfy the urge to explode. So we get emotion expressed in convulsive accents, and far too much merely loud playing.

I have often thought that every gifted pianist should play the oboe at some time in his student days so that he would learn to feel intensity without explosion. The oboe refuses to sound unless there is a controlled amount of breath used. Therefore, the oboist expresses his emotional intensity in a physical action which is associated primarily with a rhythm of following through the phrase. And here we have the secret of developing good or bad mannerisms. Mannerisms which intensify a feeling for the phrase rhythm will regulate the intensity of feeling for dynamics. But mannerisms which are associated primarily with dynamics tend to disrupt the feeling of the phrase rhythm. This is the disastrous state of affairs that makes piano playing percussive and ugly instead of graceful and beautiful.

Thus the channeling of emotions cannot be left to chance, considering the percussive nature of the instrument. The chances are all too many in favor of exploding with the hitting process.

The pianist, as well as the oboist, must get excited with his phrase rhythm—the actions called mannerisms. The expression of emotional intensity must find its outlet through the feeling for rhythmic progression. Then it is that a fusion will take place between the rhythmic line and dynamics; and only then can performance reach the heights of emotional expression.

8 Analysis of the Playing Mechanism as Related to the Use of Distance: Horizontal—Vertical—In-and-Out

Always remembering that the action for finding the key precedes the action for delivering power to the key, it behooves us to take great pains to understand fully the manner in which distance is conquered.

Since horizontal distance with the piano creates the greatest difficulties for accuracy and causes a large—very large—proportion of all the technical troubles in playing, one cannot take too much care to insure the easiest possible manipulation of this distance.

First of all, what are the possibilities in covering the width of the keyboard? They include action at every joint of the arm from shoulder to hand knuckle joint of the fingers and the joints of the thumb, plus an adjustment of the torso from the chair seat. To practice action at these joints as separate controls creates a monstrous difficulty in playing. Fortunately nature is expert in coordinating these movements; but, tragically, teaching often tears that natural coordination asunder. When it does, habits may be established which are fatal to any feeling of having conquered the difficulties of the instrument.

If one learns to play without ever having established a sense of reaching for the key position with fingers and thumb, then the torturous misery of never feeling secure with horizontal distance can be avoided, as can also the wretched experience of having to form new habits which will finally control this horizontal distance with skill.

It is this vicious habit of reaching for key position with fingers and thumb that is practically an inevitable result if and when scale-playing with finger power is used as a major tool for developing a technique. Think of the compass: the center pin without traveling any distance, just by a simple turning, controls the outside pin which travels the distance of the entire circumference of the circle. The distance is great at the periphery— nothing at all at the center. Yet the outside pin does not control the center pin—quite the reverse: the center pin controls the outside pin. Don't quibble about the differences between the simple compass and our complex machinery. Let the imagery work.

The torso is the center pin. The arm is the outside pin. They are marvelously joined by a circular joint at the shoulder. Any movement of the torso carries the arm with it. From any stance of the torso the top arm can control and instigate a movement for producing the large distance at the circumference—the keyboard. For achieving this central gauging of all action of the various levers of the arm, remember the earlier suggestion of a three-section telescope: Shove the hand into the forearm, then the forearm into the top arm, and there is left only one section —the top arm. The whole telescope fits into one cover. Then move this one section—the top arm—to control the distance of the circumference.

Or think of those umbrellas that fold up into one tiny section. The unfolding makes a large umbrella. All the joints are necessary for extending the main section into a full umbrella, but they could not operate except from the center section.

The top arm is the mighty tool for insuring easy control of horizontal distance. It is the only section of the arm which can produce a coordinated action and right balance in activity with all the other levers. Considering the actual bony structure, the skeleton forms an easier picture for understanding the controls for distance than does considering muscle action. The bones get moved about. Nature will take care of the moving process if you know which bones you want to move first. We are to deal with:

1. *Torso*—backbone standing on pelvis, which contacts the chair with the two ischial bones. Tip the pelvis over onto one bone and the backbone leans over with it. No thought process is needed for this operation, just the desire to get to the top or the bottom of the keyboard turns the trick.

2. *Top arm*—one bone, which can be moved in a complete circle and in any direction.

3. *Forearm*—two bones which, as a unit, can be flexed, folded up against the top arm, and extended into a straight line with the top arm. Or the two bones can be twisted and untwisted.

4. *Hand*—bones of the five fingers. As a rule, the hand moves in a restricted circle—not much from side to side, the movement needed for horizontal distance. The fingers can move slightly from side to side at the hand knuckle joint. The three bones of the thumb can be moved for horizontal distance. The bone connected with the wrist joint moves through the widest arc of distance.

The top arm is so skilled in its coordination with forearm flexion and extension that one hardly realizes it is the turning of its bone in the circular shoulder joint which allows the fore-

arm to function in any plane. Fold up the forearm bones so
that there is only one section of the umbrella and investigate
all these turnings. Lift, lower, look backward with it (as it
were), look forward, tip and turn in all directions. Then begin
unfolding the forearm with each new stance in the turning. See
how this allows the forearm flexion and extension to fit the
plane of horizontal distance at the keyboard. Note that this
flexion and extension of the forearm cover a large proportion
of all the horizontal distance needed. Slight—very slight—
twistings and turnings of the top arm make large actions of
the forearm available. That is the secret of easy control of horizontal distance. Never is that relationship reversed: never does
the top arm try to cover distance. It merely makes for efficient
coverage by the forearm. Only when it maintains a stance as a
fulcrum, with only slight turnings, can the forearm move with
security and expertness for wide skips in horizontal distance.
But the maintenance of that stance with its turning is the
gauge always for easy horizontal distance. Never neglect nor
ignore its quiet importance.

By untwisting the forearm bones and retwisting them, the
hand can be brought into contact with a new set of keys. The
untwist will bring the thumb perpendicularly over the little
finger. With a twist the thumb can displace the position of the
little finger on the keyboard and the hand is moved into a
fresh position. This is one of the tremendously expert means of
covering horizontal distance in arpeggios and scale playing.

There is not wide play of the hand at the wrist joint for horizontal distance, but it should never be ignored if easy horizontal distance is to be achieved. It is a part of the carry-through
to periphery, of the crack of the whip—top arm as fulcrum,
forearm snapping, propelling the hand through a distance. This
sidewise movement of the hand should by all means share horizontal distance in passing the hand over the thumb in arpeggio
and scale playing.

The sidewise play at the hand knuckle joint of the fingers is the only action of the fingers concerned with horizontal distance. Using this sidewise play should fall short of any feeling of straining to reach a position. Place the hand flat on a table and see how much sidewise action there is by each finger while three fingers remain inactive. Think this sidewise action entirely at the third joint. It can't happen elsewhere, but that fact will not necessarily prevent a struggle to assist by muscles governing the tip of the finger.

There is great variation in hands as to the amount of sidewise play with the fingers, and a small amount of such activity makes for difficulty in chord playing. The width of palm with sidewise play of fingers, not length of fingers, is the crux of easy manipulation of chords.

The thumb, by abduction and adduction of the palm segment and flexion and extension at the first two joints, adds greatly to coverage of horizontal distance. An efficient technique must utilize to the full the expertness of the thumb in this regard. This can only mean that a control utilizing the full abduction and adduction of the palm segment is achieved. Flexing the tip while achieving control of the palm segment will assist in sensing what the full control of abduction and adduction can be.

Stay away from the tips of the fingers and thumb when working for control of horizontal distance (or any other control, for that matter). Develop instead the control of this action at the center of the radius of activity, and make it an action synchronized with the action of the arm. No attention to sidewise action for horizontal distance is far better than an action which might initiate the control for that distance. The hand is always the periphery of the playing mechanism and, as such, its actions are always a follow-through—a timed and synchronized action, and never an action which is independent and on its own in controlling horizontal distance. This is imperative for any easy manipulation of the difficult skips entailed in our horizontal keyboard.

VERTICAL DISTANCE

Vertical distance in piano playing is the arc of the key-drop. Tone is produced through a down action of the key. Never think that this necessary down action is the natural prerogative of the fingers. That is one of the most damaging of all concepts for acquiring facility painlessly.

This vertical distance can be controlled by any one of the levers of the arm or shared by all of them, or any combination of them. There can be no actual dissociation of this vertical distance of the key-drop from a tone-producing power. It is, therefore, a damaging concept to localize the tone-producing power separated from the top arm, and so we must think first of the relation of top arm to this vertical distance.

Because the playing stance places the elbow slightly in front of the torso, nothing but a pull toward the torso lowers that elbow point: the down action corresponding to the key-drop.

Because action in the top arm initiates the fundamental rhythm into the playing mechanism with the follow-through activity of the torso, it is necessarily in the process of controlling the key-drop if production realizes the desired result: a total response, emotional and physical, to the aural image. A top arm controlling the key-drop for important tones can mean a top arm involved always, on the way, to taking another key-drop. No positive statement can be made as to exactly how often the top arm does control this key-drop. When playing, all the mechanics vary with tempi and the manner in which the individual feels his climaxes. But always it is the technique which utilizes every possible coordination of leverage for taking key-drop which taps the full resources of the performer—not one which isolates the action of levers, but one which uses all leverage as a synchronized unit.

If the top arm is always active in taking the key-drop of rhythmically important tones, it becomes a sort of look-out for scanning the musical horizon. That is the best possible insurance for a beautiful projection of the music. There is little danger of too many vertical actions by the top arm. There is great danger that fingers taking over will rob the top arm of this valuable control.

The forearm is a natural implement for taking vertical distance. Ask anyone to play a fast repeated action of double thirds, a sort of snare drum roll, and they will produce them with forearm taking the key-drop. Try them on an octave tremolo and they will produce it largely with rotary action. Rotary is in constant use as a sharer of the vertical distance of key-drop. No need to worry about these two actions of the forearm for taking vertical distance. If they are not forcibly ignored and annihilated by a faulty, over-active set of fingers, they will captain this distance of key-drop in fast brilliant work.

Then, when the forearm couples up with the hand, so that when it has to come up the hand is going down (alternating action), there is a tip-top combination for taking vertical distance without the small levers being overworked. This alternating action—bear it in mind—should always share the distance of key-drop with fingers in rapid passage work. Rotary action *cannot* be left out, but the alternating action unfortunately can be ignored as a blended action with fingers for taking vertical distance.

In this matter of vertical distance, try everything first—before fingers. Then let the fingers come in as it were to extend the activity of the larger levers. By no means let them usurp responsibility for the vertical key-drop.

It is center to periphery, not periphery to center, which is necessary in establishing the controls for vertical distance.

IN-AND-OUT DISTANCE

The length of the thumb, its shortness as related to the length of the fingers, plus the fact that the black keys are farther away from the body than are the white keys, demand a constant adjustment in and out for reaching key position.

Since top speed demands the least possible interference with a procedure in a straight line—horizontal line primarily—this in-and-out, or back and forth distance (and the movements controlling it), can cause havoc unless properly managed.

No in-and-out distance should be delegated to the action of fingers and thumb. That is the all-important fact to be fully realized at the outset. The fingers and thumb may play a small part in sharing this distance but they had better be ignored. Believing that they have nothing to do with the control of this movement is the only safe way to achieve an easy control.

Top arm, forearm, and hand are the levers which absorb this distance. Or, thinking in terms of joints, it is action at the shoulder, elbow and wrist which controls all in-and-out distance.

When speed is a criterion, the top arm moves in a small arc to control in-and-out distance. It acts largely as a fulcrum for the alternating action; but always it acts to cover in-and-out distance. An active, superlatively executed alternating action, which includes the "drop" and the "throw" of the hand, is the perfect counterpart of in-and-out distance. It removes all the difficulties created by the unequal length of fingers and thumb, and by having the black keys farther from the body than the white.

When a hand is small and must play an octave on the tip of the white keys, the only easy solution in playing chromatic octaves is provided by the top arm plus alternating action. Extension will be used for the black keys because they are farther away. Extension will be used with the thumb in passage work (because it can easily make up for the shortness of the thumb). In acting as a fulcrum, the top arm automatically shares the activity of the alternating action. It moves slightly back with forearm flexion, and slightly forward with forearm extension. This happens even when it is not positively motivating an in-and-out movement, but is rather standing at attention. Just the same, that movement covers some of the in-and-out distance, and how much and how continuously it performs for this distance will determine the ease in manipulating difficult passages.

9   Analysis of the Playing Mechanism as Related to the Use of Power Plus Distance: Repeated Action—Trills—Double Notes—Octaves—Arpeggios—Scales

It might be well, in this analysis of the use of power, to place in bold type at the top and bottom of the page (like advertising in a telephone directory) a line which reads, *"Most technical difficulties which persist are the result of reaching with the fingers for key position."* This reaching with the fingers practically insures the result that the fingers will act independently of the arm—they will get there first; and when they do they furnish the power for tone. Then it is that no feeling of complete efficiency in playing ever appears. Fingers have been publicized as the all-efficient tool for playing. They should be publicized as simply the periphery of the playing mechanism.

Tradition is responsible for this error. The ancestors of the piano, such as the clavichord and harpsichord, could be played with finger power, though it is very doubtful that any one of the truly great artists on these instruments ever used that power divorced from a basic rhythm. But also it is easy to believe that all but the truly great did use that power divorced from a basic rhythm, for that is what happens today.

A supremely great artist can be subjected to a traditional finger technique and still have a coordination which is integrated with a basic rhythm. But all but the very few great talents will be so damaged by this over-emphasis on finger training that they can never fulfill the talent exhibited in childhood.

Quite naturally the great artist who comes through into his full stature spends his time with music, not with the analysis of his movements in producing it. His great gifts would almost preclude his being able to analyze his own playing even if he were interested. So when he is asked to explain the prerequisites of his success, he tells the story of what he was taught—quite unaware that he is not stating a complete story of what he does.

It is like the story of the great scientist, Noguchi, explaining his experiments. So far as he was aware, he told the whole story, but he could not be aware of his natural adaptability for making all the infinitesimal movements involved in carrying out the experiments. His bodily skill defied analysis. Thus when students tried to follow his directions the experiments did not succeed. Something had been left out which was vital to the success of the experiment.

First and last, remember that only a rhythm can produce the complete coordination for playing. It alone can work the necessary magic. No analysis with words can do more than hint at the blended activity which really takes place with sensitive playing. So unless a rhythm is kindled and burns with an increasing light, there will be little assistance from an analysis of the mechanics of playing.

The top arm plus the torso kindles the rhythm. Unless the mechanics of tone production are completely synchronized with this rhythm, they will remain mechanics unrelated to the actual blended activity which produces successful playing. The torso acts as a fulcrum for the arm which is the equipment for delivering power to the key.

In making this analysis it is taken for granted that rhythmic grace with top speed and power are the goals to be attained; for if they are achieved there will be a mechanism which is adequate for a pianissimo and beautiful melody playing.

The manner in which a repeated action (doing the same thing over again with a lever) is used, becomes a determining factor for speed, brilliance, greatest possible ease, skilled manipulation of dynamics, and subtlety in rhythmic nuance. Therefore, if this statement is true, it is this repeated action which assists or hampers all the desirable attributes of playing.

A repeated action is necessarily in constant use if brilliance with speed is achieved, for it happens automatically except when fingers alone are being used for tone production. Fingers alone never produce brilliance with speed or speed with brilliance. It takes the total playing mechanism to achieve that.

It is the manner in which a repeated action is used which avoids a note-wise progression and establishes listening habits that attend to a musical unit rather than to one tone at a time.

A repeated action, properly used, always absorbs the production of at least one tone during its process of repetition—while it is taking place. This means a smaller lever tucks in a tone while a larger lever is repeating its action.

A note-wise procedure means a separate use of power for each tone—exactly what is achieved by independent fingers producing the tone. No note-wise progression can duplicate in beauty what a phrase-wise progression achieves.

This repeated action takes place with top arm, forearm, and hand. Or saying the same thing another way, at shoulder, elbow and wrist. (Note the absence of fingers.) The *top arm* repeated action initiates the basic rhythm as it is associated with the important tones of a phrase. It takes the key-drop and produces the power for those important tones. While its repetition is taking place, the forearm, hand, or fingers tuck in the modifiers of the phrase, the less important tones.

The *forearm* is the natural implement for a fast repeated action and its action is the central control for fast articulation. Its repeated action is always associated with the action of hand and fingers. That is, the hand and fingers operate inside its repeated action—while it is going on.

The *hand's* repeated action, which is desirable for performance, is the part it plays in the alternating action. The alternating action, plus rotary, should always share production with fingers. The fingers play inside the hand's repeated action—with it—while it is taking place.

This relationship in repeated action *is* the blended action which produces all beautiful playing: top arm absorbing forearm, forearm absorbing hand, alternating action (forearm and hand) plus rotary absorbing fingers.

The following example will serve to indicate the tremendous advantage of a repeated action which absorbs another action during its repetition. The entire analysis will deal with this principle.

Ill. 6

Here are four articulations. Each requires a down action because tone is produced by a vertical key-drop. Each down action by the same lever demands a coming-up action as preparation for the down action.

Produce the four octaves with the down action of the forearm. Play them fast. It feels fast. The coming-up actions are non-productive of tone. Now, as the forearm flexes (the coming-up action), flex the hand (the down action). The down action of the hand can produce G while the forearm is coming up: getting ready to produce G♯. Four tones for two repeated actions will be the result, instead of four repeated actions for four tones—the same speed of tones (or faster) for half the speed in repetition. That is the simple truth. That is the answer to playing which is tremendously fast and yet does not seem tremendously difficult. One salient fact in dealing with the repeated action is the constant motivation involved in the top arm. Remember the formula: top arm absorbs forearm; forearm absorbs hand; alternating action plus rotary absorbs fingers. Nothing will work out right if the activity in the top arm is ignored. It will be established habits of reaching with the fingers which will prevent the formula from working, and under these circumstances there never will be any sense of mastery of the instrument.

The involvement of the top arm can easily be sensed by playing this very fast rhythmic pattern of double thirds:

Ill. 7

Make it sound like the rattattattoo of the woodpecker, or the roll of the snare drum. If it comes off with gusto, it will be produced in just one manner. No instruction is needed, for there is only one easy and efficient way to accomplish this. Any way except with the forearm taking the key-drop is too difficult. The forearm will always take over for a fast brilliant repeated action of short duration. It cannot keep the speed of the snare drum roll going for any length of time without the playing feeling strained and difficult, but the short roll will feel easy and efficient, and can be very fast. Do it a number of times and then observe the top arm. What is happening there? By no stretch of the imagination can it be called inactive. It is almost violently involved. It will practically take over the production of the last tone and it certainly takes care of the first. And in between it is actively involved in staying down and acting as a fulcrum for the activity of the forearm. It has its own repeated action, but it does not take care of consecutive tones. It takes care of the important rhythmic tones.

The trouble is that when the speed involved in this rattat-tattoo is not present and the demand for cooperation is not so great and obvious, the top arm is all too frequently ignored and allowed to be less involved in production of the power for tone. It should always be the tap root for the power in playing. When it is, the necessary attributes for beauty can all be synchronized. Without it, all playing is less adequate and less productive of sensitivity in the use of power—the dynamics for phrase modeling.

OCTAVE TRILL

A trill produced with the cooperation of top arm and forearm will not only be a thing of beauty and a joy forever, but it will serve to enhance the beauty and ease of all fluent passage work. That is certainly not true of a trill produced with finger

Ill. 8

power. The latter is difficult and requires constant attention to keep it in order; and it never fits graciously into the curves of the music or promotes fluent passage work. Worst of all, it leads to note-wise listening.

The trill is a musical pattern which is never found ready-made except with a real playing talent. When it is found, there is no need to doubt that here, so far as technique is concerned, is a big gift.

If traditional teaching had only observed a talented eight-year-old trilling and adopted his manner of trilling, all the rest of us might have been saved a vast amount of unproductive labor. Unproductive not only because a finger trill is the hardest means of trilling, but because it breeds habits both in listening and playing which are detrimental to rhythmic grace. A finger trill means a note-wise procedure and note-wise listening. That is the fundamental reason for discarding it.

There is economy in effort if the single trill is produced with the same habits of action which are a necessity for the octave trill. More than that, it is an effort which is a constructive factor in furthering a blended activity, right for all musical patterns, and for listening habits conducive to beautiful phrase modeling.

Certainly a single trill can be played with fingers and beautifully played. It is to be observed in use by many artists. It is also to be observed that there is no consistency in their manner of playing the single trill. But there is consistency in the manner in which these same artists will play the octave trill.

What does that mean? Simply that there is only one way this octave trill can be played with efficiency. Using only a part of the whole arm mechanism for playing is inadequate to produce the octave trill. It takes the blended activity of the entire arm.

Since a blended activity is demanded for virtuoso playing, if it can be started on its way and helped to perfection by the trill, great economy in time and effort can be achieved by using the trill. The fact that the trill demands the utmost in subtle blending because of its compactness, makes for efficiency in starting with it. It also makes a demand for thorough understanding of what goes into virtuoso playing. If one can effectively start a blended activity with a trill, it is an excellent place to start. The same combination of leverage can be used for all trills and for all playing, but always there will be a variance in the proportion of activity between the octave trill and the single trill. It is this variance which causes the confusion in ideas concerning the method of trilling. This same variance is a major factor in acquiring all technical facility. But if a blended activity is the corner-stone of all the habits acquired, then ears and rhythm have a chance to take care of this variance in leverage. This defies any factual analysis but it can be suggested.

The reason for using the trill at the beginning of the analysis of power is to establish a repeated action: a repeated action attached to the primary tone of the trill, while the other tone is tucked in by a different lever, or, rather, levers. The primary tone is simply the tone which starts the trill. In the octave trill it is reinforced—the octave adds to its rhythmic importance. This repeated action is easily thwarted by the habit of note-wise listening, supposing there has been an established trill with fingers. That is, the trill will neither feel like a repeated action nor will you attend to it as such. It will remain two tones of equal importance, produced by separate initiations of power. If it is argued that the two tones *should* be of equal importance, there is only one answer: listen to the artist play this trill and see whether you attend to it as two tones of equal importance or whether you attend to it as a rhythmic musical pattern.

Playing the trill as a repeated action does not require unequal dynamics in producing the two tones—the trill need not sound uneven. It must, of course, be a beautiful trill, have evenness in dynamics and spacing; but also it must be an embellishment creating beauty. That can mean only one thing: that it does not stop the flow in progression of the musical idea it is embellishing. Certainly the flow in progression, musically, cannot include note-wise listening nor note-wise progression physically —nor an interruption to the basic rhythm—without being damaged. These are the real reasons why the trill should be produced with a repeated action which absorbs one tone into its repetition. It can foster the repeated action which is necessary for all beautiful playing.

For this very reason, never treat the trill as mechanics. Treat it as a very beautiful adornment—use it as a part of the rhythm of the phrase pattern as a whole. Let perfecting it into equal spacing and equality in intensity of tone production come after the rhythmic repetition has been established.

Rhythm first is always a necessity for the final accomplishment of satisfying results in every instance, musical or technical. The full arm makes the initial contact with the keyboard, assuming the playing stance. In the discussion of the trill, principal tone or first tone simply indicates the tone which starts the trill. The three trills used will illustrate the repeated actions of top arm and forearm in relation to the principal tones and the tucked-in tones.

The combination of top arm, forearm, hand, and fingers works to fold up or lengthen out the arm. In this process, some levers are coming up while others are going down. It takes a down action to contact tone. Up actions are negative so far as taking the key-drop is concerned, but they are positive in implementing the down action.

It is exactly in relation to this reciprocal kind of action, the forearm throwing the hand into action, for instance, that the wrist joint is so spectacularly efficient. There must be movement by the hand which is dominated by the forearm—that is, there must be the combination of activity whereby a tiny fast movement produces a movement through a wider arc, for conservation in the use of distance and power. It is like the relation of the whip handle to the tip which snaps. For the pianist, this relationship is between forearm and hand.

This involves the so-called "loose wrist." The trouble with talking about a loose wrist is that it does not indicate the necessary vitality elsewhere which makes the looseness effective. Looseness at the wrist is no virtue except as it is in operation with a vital action—then it is a necessity for extending a small action into a larger action, and to allow powerful muscles to produce a large proportion of the power for tone.

The top arm is the central control for the entire coordination of power. The forearm is the center of the control for an articulation which possesses both speed and brilliance. It is the action of repetition of these two large levers that dominates a technique which possesses real virtuosity.

The top arm and forearm are the positive arbiters of power in playing the piano. They can take all the strain out of playing if they are properly used. If this repeated action is clearly understood in relation to these trills, a mechanism can be established which will function throughout the entire gamut of playing patterns. Never lose sight of the fact that in trilling only a fraction of the distance of the key-drop is used. Increase that distance unnecessarily and nothing will work with dexterity. The key is never allowed to come up to its top level. It comes up only far enough to make another tone possible. If the power of the top arm is balanced against the resistance of the key action at just the level where the hammer trips, it can be used through a very tiny arc of distance. This is a necessity for its efficient use with speed.

Top arm initiates and maintains the control of level for all trilling, as it does for all virtuoso playing. This is partially imagery, for the top arm is dependent upon the forearm, hand and fingers for maintaining contact with the key. But it is imagery very closely related to fact.

It is the sensing of level with top arm which is present when the top arm acts as a fulcrum for the forearm. Either the top arm is taking key-drop and producing tone, or it is maintaining the level and gauging the action of the lever or levers which are actively taking the key-drop.

The glissando is the best possible illustration of this maintaining of level by the top arm.

Have this control of level by the top arm a vivid reality before trying the octave trill.

When one says up and down for key action, or arm action, it is easy to think a definite up action or a definite down action. There is no such feeling in this up and down involved in using power at key resistance. The actions are so tiny and so dove-

tailed that all one feels is an active alertness to keep the key
between its top and bottom levels. It is this kind of subtle up
and down balance with which the top arm activates its control
in trilling.

With this balancing there is activity at all the joints. This
activity is of two kinds: creating a unified bony structure for
power to play against, or reversal in action at some joints so
that the key can come up.

This interplay of vitalization using reversal of action at various joints is the basis of expert trilling. It will sound crude and
is crude in the analysis. In actual performance it is of infinite
subtlety. Observe the glissando: the relation of the vitality in
the pull of the top arm to the play in activity at the hand
knuckle joint of the finger. One cannot think that activity of
finger. It is just there in relating the power of the arm to the
key-drop. It is absolutely necessary but it is a complementary
action. It is not the positive power which is producing the glissando. There is that kind of relationship to the power of the
top arm in all virtuoso playing. The periphery assists but it does
not initiate, independently of arm. Keep track of the repeated
action of the top arm and forearm. Never let them go by default
because the fingers become too active.

No one knows any better than I do that making that suggestion isn't going to cure fingers of doing more than their share
in trilling. And only when they are cured of independence and
learn to assist rather than to initiate will these trills, involving
a repeated action of top arm and forearm, operate with fluency
and brilliance.

Ask any small boy to show you his muscle. He will violently
flex his forearm. Note how automatically the top arm is involved. It pulls toward the torso and is just as active as the forearm.

This pull of the top arm with flexion of the forearm is the
clue to the trill. Flexion with the forearm does not produce the
down action which is necessary for tone production, but it is a

component part of the pull of top arm and flexion of the hand which do produce the down action necessary for contacting tone. The hand can only go down in relation to the forearm as the forearm is raised, because there is a fixed level at the keyboard at which the hand always operates. The pull of the top arm is always involved with the level at which tone is produced. Use this pull of top arm with the flexion of the hand, and the flexion of the forearm as the connecting link, for producing the octave of the trill. Repeat the octave with this combination of leverage. Then, while this repetition is taking place, tuck in the single tone with extension of the forearm, with finger action (flexion at hand knuckle joint) synchronized with forearm extension, plus rotary action. If the single tone is produced with this combination of leverage there is no lack of power for producing a tone of equal intensity to that produced with the other combination of top arm, hand and forearm. At this stage refer to the goal of developing and utilizing the repeated action.

If rotary is allowed too wide a play in its combination with finger action, it will easily and almost surely exclude the forearm extension. Exclude the latter, and the combined leverage for the repeated octave will be displaced. The octave will also be produced with rotary and fingers. Rotary never makes the same demand on top arm sharing that the alternating action makes. This is the grievous lack when it is allowed too much responsibility. Put the responsibility squarely on the alternating action and rotary will add its expert skill. This is of great importance. Too much rotary action will produce a tone-wise listening, the very thing which must be avoided for all beautiful playing.

All trills should feel like a repeated action and be listened to as a repeated action. Keep the combination for producing the octave a vivid sensation, and achieve its repetition until the single tone can be tucked in without in the least interrupting the physical sensation of repeating the octave.

Then never forget the all-important factor of rhythm. Never

put too much faith in mechanics. It is a rhythm which always turns the trick. *Use the trill, feel it and listen to it as a repeated action, as part of a musical idea.* If it is needed to round out the musical statement and to heighten its dramatic effect (and not felt and listened to as separate tones), it will be absorbed into the rhythmic progression of the phrase. It is only when a compelling rhythm manipulates the combination of leverage— actually forces a blended activity in order to produce the desired results within the musical framework—that all the requirements for playing this trill come into being.

SINGLE TRILL

The difference in the way an octave trill and a single trill is produced is enormous in most instances, as one observes them in virtuoso performances. This difference furnishes an excellent example of the great dichotomy which exists between the activity which is taught and the activity which is actually necessary for top performance. The octave trill cannot be successfully played except as the whole mechanism is involved, so every talented person just uses the whole mechanism when it is demanded, with complete disregard for the teaching. The results turn out to be uniform. The octave trill can only be accomplished with brilliance and speed when the top arm and alternating action are producing the expert use of power for tone. But the single trill is a different matter. It can be played with the fingers, in accordance with traditional training, and thus the teaching will take. Once it does and the trill is produced with finger control, it is the most difficult of all playing habits to supplant with a repeated action. The ears have listened always two tones; they will see to it that by hook or crook a separate initiation of power for each tone is achieved. They have learned to listen with these individual initiations of power by the fingers. They can only change that kind of listening habit once there is a production which will absorb at least one tone while another is being produced—a repeated action.

But how to establish that repeated action in spite of all the physical habits of production by fingers plus note-wise listening habits—that is the question. Of course the answer is that production gets involved with rhythmic progression. But saying that is certainly not going to make a dent in any of the trilling habits. In fact, nothing will do any good except a conviction that any kind of misery is worth the effort if note-wise listening can be thwarted: knowing that if note-wise listening persists in any crook or cranny of the playing mechanism it can easily spread like mustard in a wheat field to the entire area.

Perhaps the most efficient manner of achieving a single trill with the same repeated action which is demanded by the octave trill, is to slip up on it unawares by doing something else which is closely related. Find an attractive composition with fast repeated double thirds and learn to play it with a luscious rhythmic grace. Make it a thing of beauty because a basic rhythm makes it melt and run in a smooth lilting fashion. Then one day, without damaging that lilting rhythm in the slightest degree, open the double thirds—that is, sound the two tones singly instead of as a third.

The Shostakovich Prelude, Op. 34, No. 15 has worked in this manner. A pupil happened to be playing it and had achieved a rhythmic grace in performance. All efforts to master the trill with a repeated action had failed—the fingers always took over. One day, without warning, I asked her to open the thirds (in the middle of a performance). The blended repeated action held and there was the trill just one key removed. The next time we tampered with the Prelude and used seconds instead of thirds, and when they were opened the trill appeared. It took some time to carry over into trilling, but eventually it did.

For learning the details of production with a repeated action, an excerpt from the Chopin Etude, Op. 25, No. 3 is useful:

Ill. 9a

Once achieved with a repeated action, it means a beginning. It does not necessarily mean success in transferring the sensation directly to a trill. But eventually, if there is sufficient belief in the importance of possessing a trill with a repeated action in order thoroughly to choke out note-wise listening, a connection can be made. This trill with the new repeated action will neither feel expert nor sound even and brilliant for a long time. It will just be a thorn in the flesh. But the fact will remain—a trill with a repeated action can be both beautiful and easy to play; and when it is accomplished it lends itself in a marvelous fashion as an embellishment, for there will be no note-wise listening to it. It will enhance the rhythm of the phrase.

What's more, there are artists who use this trill with the repeated action consistently. If there were not, I should never have found it. I learned it from hearing it and seeing it in a very beautiful performance by one of the world's greatest artists. There is a great deal of variance in the blend of the repeated action between this single trill and the octave trill, but the basic factors are the same and all the same elements are present in both. There is simply a freer play of movement for the single trill.

The repeated action at the elbow throws the hand in such a manner that the repeated action of the hand is very obvious. It will not work, however, if the repeated action is initiated at the wrist. What happens at the wrist is a follow-through of the action initiated at the elbow. That is important to remember.

(For this relationship, go back and investigate the snap, page 28.) See to it that the hand moves easily in response to a quick action at the elbow, but make it the periphery of that action —like the ripple caused by dropping a pebble into a pool. The top arm and alternating action go into play, and the hand and fingers follow through.

In all first attempts *avoid a legato trill*; fingers can take over too easily when legato is in use. One reason for success in using this pattern for observing the detailed action is that it is not too difficult to avoid legato in a moderate tempo.

The habits to be supplanted are:

a. Fingers taking key-drop and producing the power for tone.

b. Too wide a rotary action.

These are the actions which produce note-wise listening. The habits to be established are:

a. Taking key-drop with top arm for tones rhythmically important.

b. Using alternating action to take care of fast articulation.

c. Finger action synchronized with the alternating action.

d. Rotary used compactly in a small arc.

e. Power for tone entirely furnished by top arm and alternating action—not by fingers and rotary. (This statement, if not completely factual, is excellent imagery for the desired result: a blended action.)

First achieve the speed of a real performance with the pattern reduced. Make the melody dance and sing—have fun with it as a delightfully rhythmic tune:

Ill. 9b

Repeated action of the top arm takes the melody tunes. Repeated action at elbow plays the double seconds. The wrist is free and allows the hand to be thrown into vibration by the fast repetition at the elbow.

Note that the 32nd notes have become 16ths. Note also that there is no legato in the playing of the repeated seconds. There never is a regulation legato (the key held down until the second tone is sounded) with a repeated action. This non-legato produces a distinctive difference in the feeling of a trill with a repeated action, as opposed to the legato feeling of the trill with finger action. It always disappears the minute the fingers take over for the trill. So one of the positive means for developing the trill with repeated action is to become vividly aware of the sensation of non-legato with the repeated action.

When the pattern is slowed down for a detailed analysis of the movements involved, exaggerate the non-legato by using a snap for the second 16th. (Refer to page 28 for snap.) This exaggeration cannot be maintained when there is speed in trilling but it will help to insure that the repeated action is maintained when this pattern is opened into the trill.

We now have two repeated actions from elbow playing the repeated 16th—two down actions with the forearm. With these down actions, there is each time a drop of the hand, because as a preparation for the down action there is the up action of the forearm, which automatically swings the hand up a bit if the wrist is free and not holding the hand in a rigid relationship with the forearm.

Fuss with this repeated action at the elbow and the follow-through vibration of the hand until it is a simple reaction to have the hand tremble, like a leaf on the end of a stem, when the forearm uses a fast repeated action. This relationship in activity must be a reality for a trill produced with a repeated action. The repeated action of the forearm *produces* the repeated action of the hand. Power is created with the repeated action at the elbow and is transmitted to the key through a repeated action at the wrist, which includes the bones of the fingers.

Remembering the up action involved in all this repeated action, now put a tone into it, by letting the rotary action plus finger take the key-drop for C, while the flexion—the up action of forearm—is taking place.

Now is the time when the trouble begins—the moment a finger shares the distance of key-drop. Fingers were not in use until now except as bones to stand under the power of the arm; but once they are allowed action, the repeated action of forearm and hand will probably disappear. It is no easy task to deny the fingers the power for tone and yet allow them individual play.

Here we are dealing with habits which can easily mean a Waterloo for this trill with a repeated action. The way out is filled with underbrush, and patience is a first prerequisite if success is to be achieved.

As always, the real solution will tie up with a rhythm which possesses an emotional response to beautiful music. Just don't open the trill in a hurry. Use Bach and Scarlatti, which are full of trills. Each time one appears, simply play a rhythmic repeated action, using the two tones of the trill as a double second. Until the repeated action is a natural response to bumping into a trill, the trill cannot be opened with success. But if patience has lasted long enough and the repeated action does jump to take over at the sign of a trill, the day will arrive when the trill can be opened without the fingers' taking over and annihilating the repeated action.

It is actually the rotary action more than the fingers which opens the trill—at least it should be. There is no shifting rotary action while the repeated action plays against a double second. When the rotary begins to twist and untwist, the power of the arm is channeled in favor of first one and then the other. With this whole equipment of repeated action and rotary, the action of the finger is a buckling under the power so that only one finger at a time keeps vitalized to receive the power. It is not a positive action by the finger to take the key-drop: that is the real difficulty. It is no trick to have the finger action synchronized with the rotary action—that is natural and easy. The trick is to have their willing cooperation and not have them destroy the repeated action.

There is practically no relation in sensation of the trill with a repeated action and a trill with fingers. So if the trill feels natural, observe whether the repeated action has disappeared. Not until the repeated action feels natural when trilling can it be trusted to remain in command for this trill.

The violinist's trill is a repeated action by a finger. While the finger lifts in order to go down again, the string sounds during that lift. Listen to the spinning of that trill. The pianist's trill will open also when produced with a repeated action, for it means that one of the tones will be tucked in while the other is being repeated.

Once the repeated action becomes the natural response to trilling, the trill loses its difficulties—just as there was no difficulty in playing a fast repeated roll of double thirds.

As nearly as one can indicate the difference in balance in activity between the octave trill and the single trill, it is this: the strongest positive activity, the power-producing activity, lies in the pull of the top arm for the octave trill. The repeated action which is most obvious, which is the strongest feeling, is the repeated action of the top arm. The repeated action which is most obvious for the single trill is that of the forearm throwing the hand into the movement.

No easy blend of these necessary movements will take place unless the power for tone is balanced against the key action at the level where tone is produced—or rather where the hammer trips to produce the tone (practically keyed). The feel of the balance of the key is never allowed to be interrupted. The key is never allowed to come up to its top level. It is allowed to come up just enough to make another tone possible. This is imperative. It means that the smallest arc of vertical distance for tone production is being used.

THE TRILL IN
DOUBLE THIRDS

The repeated action for a trill in double thirds involves still another balance in activity. First of all, two fingers must operate with a single purpose, as a unit, to transmit the power of the top arm and the forearm with exact precision in timing. In achieving this precision in control, it is the easiest thing in the world to let the two fingers take over too much responsibility for both the distance of key-drop and the power for tone. When and if this happens, nothing but an eight-hours-a-day schedule of practice will offer any solution to the difficulties involved; and not even then will there be an easy spinning of this trill.

Secondly, practically all rotary action is shut out, and that puts an added burden elsewhere. Rotary tilts the hand and that tilting makes for difficulty in the precision of the third. It is easier to maintain the third—to keep two fingers equalized in length under the palm—than it is to adjust that length for each third, which is necessary if the rotary action tilts the palm.

Let *imagery*, *sensation* and *rhythm* take over. They will accomplish what no amount of analysis and practice with fingers can.

For *imagery*, believe that the fingers contribute not the slightest atom of power for tone. Believe that the thirds are produced with everything except fingers.

For *sensation*, use the exact same feeling of the repeated action in the top arm—the same pull with the third which starts the trill—as was used for the starting octave in the octave trill.

For *rhythm*, use a musical pattern which involves a phrase-wise procedure. Desire the lilt of the phrase which makes for grace in musical projection more than you desire a perfect trill. The listening must not be note-wise for this difficult trill any more than for the other trills.

DOUBLE NOTES, THIRDS, FOURTHS, SIXTHS

For all the same reasons that a trill in double thirds is difficult, so are passages in double notes, fourths and sixths. The *difficulties* are:

1. Note-wise procedure.
2. Reaching with fingers. This reaching will fill in the time space between tones with activity in the movements of articulation—which should never happen.
3. Two fingers acting as a unit.
4. More power is needed to produce two tones than one.
5. Rotary action is not available.
6. Passing is made difficult because the adjustment to the new position is slightly retarded and has to be made all at once. (The position for producing the tones must be maintained longer than one for producing a single tone.)

Remedies are as follows:

1. Use rhythm of the musical idea. Do not put attention on individual initiations of power.
2. Find position with top arm—the only efficient deterrent to reaching with fingers. If top arm gauges distance it will also fill in the time unit between tones, and by so doing it can implement the basic rhythm.
3. Do not relax the adjustment of one set of fingers while the other set is functioning. Maintain a readiness by having two bones always alerted to receive the power from the strong levers.
4. Extra power needed for producing two tones is provided by top arm and forearm—never, never, never by fingers.
5. Make up for the lack of rotary by having a very active alternating action.
6. Nowhere is the advantage greater for having a small action produce an action of greater width than in this passing of

double notes. The hand is thrown into position by a quick action at the elbow.

Use the productive chromatic octave pattern (Illustration 1, page 34) for getting a vivid sensation of the natural manner in which the top arm assumes the control of horizontal distance —the finding of the keys to be played. Then use *exactly* the same kind of adjustment when there is not a chromatic passage to bring the top arm automatically into that kind of play. (This will be discussed in "Octaves," which follows, and also in the chapter on "Learning with a Rhythm.")

Words will never be adequate for expressing the difference between a balance of action which relieves small muscles and a balance in action which burdens small muscles. The difference in ease and freedom is tremendous even though the power added to small muscles is slight.

It is because almost inevitably, when an added amount of power delivered for tone is given over to fingers, this power is coupled with a reaching for key position and keybed. This in turn prevents action at periphery from being coordinated with the full arm. Then note-wise listening appears and the next disaster is a loss of the fundamental rhythm. The entire playing mechanism is thrown out of gear for speed and brilliance, to say nothing of what happens to the beauty of production.

The greatest insurance against acquiring difficulties instead of virtuosity in practicing double notes is a fundamental rhythm which will produce phrase-wise listening.

OCTAVES

Octaves are only more of the same. Because of the span, they can cause even more disturbance than the thirds and sixths. If there is capacity for fluency in passage work and there is a possible octave span in the hand, then there is capacity for fluent octaves. If they are not fluent, that is due to perfectly concrete factors which can be changed.

If these factors are not changed and there is substituted instead a rigorous work-out each day to increase endurance, the octaves will never quite rise to virtuosity. Ironing in a faulty habit—"perfecting one's mistakes," as Auer put it—by hours of drill is never the actual solution to technical problems. Remove the cause of the difficulty, which is always a faulty manipulation of distance and power, and then practice will produce results. The causes for lack of results with octaves will almost surely lie in some combination of the following habits:

1. A faulty manner of holding the span.
2. A reaching for key position with fingers and hand.
3. A localizing of the power for tone with action at the wrist.
4. A bearing down in the forearm.

It may take consistent attention for a time to supplant these habits by the right ones, but it certainly can be done. Right habits can be just as definite as faulty ones. The only difference is that there are many ways to be wrong in the use of power for distance and tone, and so far as I know there is only one principle which will make all things right. That is the use of two powerful levers—top arm and forearm—for initiating the controls for distance and power. Any habits which block the controls with these levers will certainly prevent virtuosity with octaves.

That is exactly what happens with the above-mentioned faulty habits. The corrections are actually simple, but habits are so extraordinarily subtle and evasive in their operation that the corrections never get a chance really to function. Here they are:

1. The faulty span is one which reaches and holds at the *tips* of thumb and finger. All that is needed to cure that habit is to achieve the holding of the span between the hand knuckles of the finger and the second joint of the thumb. That means opening the palm instead of stretching the fingers.

Learn to abduct the thumb with the palm segment. It is quite easy to localize this control if the thumb is flexed at the first and second joints. Once it is localized then all that is needed is practice to make the control expert.

To avoid reaching with the tips of the fingers, keep the fingers relaxed at the hand knuckle—let them drop—while the palm is opened and the thumb is abducted. The result should be a kind of diagonal pull from hand knuckle joint of finger to second joint of thumb. When this is achieved, then extend the fingers and thumb. Let their straightening out simply extend the action in the palm, as the baton extends the arm of the conductor. Their extension should in no way initiate the action for taking the span—that is the secret of an easy octave span. Good imagery for achieving the same result is to use a full arm stroke against the fifth finger, and hold that key down. Then aim with the upper arm for the key an octave away.

Completely ignore the fact that there must be action in the hand in order to achieve the octave span. Just let the top arm take over. That will produce a minimum of activity in the hand, which is the desired result. Thinking action back of where it must take place is always a good practice for making adjustment to horizontal distance. Trying to be literal is no virtue. Results are what count, and since it is not possible to analyze with accuracy the blended activity necessary for perfection, all devices of imagery provide the best way of getting results.

Fluent octaves must have a span taken in the palm and not at the tips of fingers.

2. When it comes to reaching for position with fingers and hand, I confess to a somewhat hopeless feeling about having any explanation to cure that insidious and destructive habit. It persists and persists like dandelions in a lawn.

Reaching with fingers *can* be cured, but only by achieving a very active top arm and forearm. That is the crux of solving the mechanics of playing octaves, and actually of all virtuosity.

It is the action of the top arm which both taps the greatest source of power and implements a rhythm; and it can only function for these factors if it controls the finding of the key. The key must be found before tone can be produced. Only when the top arm is involved in finding the key will activity between tones take place with the fundamental rhythm—a necessity for subtlety in spacing tones and beautiful playing.

The simplest and easiest manner of sensing this action of top arm that I have found after a long search is a pattern of chromatic octaves:

Ill. 10

etc.

Slip into playing them right in the middle of doing the skipping octave pattern. In that way you will have attention on a full arm stroke—top arm in complete control of production. That will mean an advantageous start. In playing the straight chromatic run from F♯ to A♯, note the activity of the top arm. You will find that quite naturally it initiates the action for finding position. It takes the initiative for the in-and-out distance, and in the process moves over the keys to be played. Note also that there is slight awareness of the action which takes the key-drop. This unawareness of vertical action only happens when the top arm is sliding into position for each succeeding tone.

The minute the hand takes over and prepares for position there is an awareness that the playing feels fast and difficult, and the up and down action is increased. *The top arm, even with consecutive white keys, finds the succeeding keys with the same kind of activity with which it plays the chromatic pattern.*

What about the horizontal keyboard and the straight line that is the shortest distance between two points? The answer is that slight indentures in that straight line, taken by the top arm, produce far less disturbance in fluency than any exaggeration in the vertical action. The minute the top arm is not actively involved in finding the key, the levers responsible for articulation (producing the vertical action for key-drop) will also absorb the control for horizontal progression (finding succeeding keys). Any virtuosity achieved under these circumstances will take an enormous amount of practice and probably produce a hampering strain in the forearm.

Any solution, imagery or other types, which makes vivid the fact that all the activity between tones should be concerned with the process of finding the key position with the top arm, is most valuable. For example, imagine the keys are far apart and act as little trap doors. They can be sprung only when the top arm comes along as it controls horizontal progression. Or, still thinking the distance between keys as very large, think a slow progression toward each key, like a slow motion picture, with top arm actively in control, and with definiteness become aware that the fingers and hand are idle (not reaching out) during this process. Make them wait until the last split second, as the top arm slips them into key position, before they are allowed to function at all for taking the key-drop.

When they do function they are the periphery of the action taken with the forearm.

3. Believing that octaves are played from the wrist is similar to the belief that the fingers produce power for tone in passage work. The greatest assistance in losing this belief is the inability to achieve virtuosity when it is put into practice.

True, one sees an active hand when octaves are being played. If the attention were directed to forearm and top arm, greater activity would be seen there also. It is simply that the width of the play of the hand is greater than the width of the movement of top arm and forearm. So, as noted before, the tip of the whip moves in a wider arc of distance than the handle. But the tip does not boss the handle activity. Neither does the hand boss the activity for octaves. It is a part of the blended activity which starts with top arm finding the key, and forearm taking the initiative for key-drop. Sometimes, of course, the top arm does take the key-drop; it does this for special accents.

The manner in which the repeated action of the two powerful levers dovetails their movements is the solution to virtuosity with octaves. Think about it and then watch a virtuoso octave passage played by an authoritative pianist.

4. A bearing down in the forearm will mean a fairly consistently low wrist. It will be the complement of octaves motivated at the wrist. And it will be an action not produced as a blended cooperating movement with the top arm, but one in which the forearm will act only as a fulcrum for the hand. This is never the coordination which produces virtuosity with octaves or anything else.

There can be no argument concerning the need for powerful muscles to be involved with the production of octaves which have velocity and brilliance. Well, then these powerful muscles which control action in top arm and forearm must *instigate* the controls which involve the less powerful muscles of the hand and fingers. It cannot be the other way around.

The natural action of the forearm which implements the pull of the top arm is an up action—not a bearing down. Then when the top arm is not producing the full power for tone (but simply finding—gauging—position and acting as a fulcrum for the forearm), the forearm goes into positive motion for taking the key-drop and producing tone.

With quick repeated actions, the forearm throws the hand

out and down. The hand is as much a part of its action as a
leaf which trembles is part of its stem. This fast repeated action
of forearm automatically involves the top arm as fulcrum. It
also will never be done naturally without a "snugging *up*" to
the top arm. This snugging up is the opposite of bearing down
in the forearm.

Speed in this repeated action will shorten the distance from
shoulder to tip of fingers. It is never achieved by a lengthening
out of that distance. The bearing down action belongs to the
lengthening process, not to the shortening one. Bearing down
can easily make the playing of brilliant octaves an impossibility.

It is never safe to say, in a given musical pattern, that the top
arm takes the key-drop for certain tones, and the forearm with
alternating action takes exactly so many tones in between.
Rhythm and tempo and emotion are the determining factors
for a real performance. But it *is* safe to say that the top arm
and forearm activity—the amount and dovetailing of their actions—will determine whether octaves feel possible and are
played brilliantly. If a passage feels difficult, look to the top
arm. See whether it is motivating the control for key position,
filling in between tones (the preparation for producing succeeding tones), and actually producing the power for important
tones.

Unless the top arm is in active control of horizontal distance,
it can be too static to implement a basic rhythm. That is when
the hope for top beauty and virtuosity in performance can be
abandoned.

ARPEGGIOS

The desirable result in arpeggio playing is that there should be
no bumps in dynamics and that fluency *with accuracy* should be
counted on. No one is comfortable with accuracy one day and
inaccuracy the next. If only it were possible to make it clear to
everyone that inaccuracy with a talented player is the result of

a faulty adjustment for the control of distance in about ninety percent of the instances, instead of an insufficient amount of detailed practice, then this book would be worth the effort.

A talented player is one with an auditory control of action. That is, movement is made to find the tone the ear desires to hear. This talent will have either absolute pitch or a very reliable relative pitch, and an excellent natural coordination, which always means a rhythmic gift.

All playing of professional caliber is produced *with* these assets—not without them.

The capacity for accuracy is a part of this equipment. When inaccuracy persists in a certain passage, it is because there is a faulty adjustment. If that were not true why wouldn't the difficult passage succumb to practice? The same passage does not trouble another player.

Slow practice, shifting accents, making a variety of exercises out of a detail—not any of these usually applied remedies removes the hazard entirely. It is reasonable that they should fail for the actual cause is not removed before the practice takes place. The chances are that if the cause for the inaccuracy were removed, the extra practice would never need to take place.

Horizontal distance must be correctly taken if accuracy is reliable; and arpeggios, involving a width in this distance, very quickly unearth difficulties where there is a faulty control.

The well-established concept of a key legato in passing cannot escape doing inestimable damage in playing arpeggios. If there is persistent belief that what we hear as legato playing on the piano means the literal holding of one key until the next is played, then nothing can be done about weeding out the difficulties of arpeggio playing.

There cannot be a propitious handling of horizontal distance, and with it an even and easy delivery of power for successive tones, if a key legato in passing the thumb and hand is made an important issue. This legato in passing has no point except to hamper progression.

What is actually the crucial point for beautiful arpeggios is a power applied evenly to successive keys so that there will be no bumps in dynamics to prevent a flow of smoothly graded tones —the real basis for the legato feeling in fluent piano playing.

Realistic listening is all that is necessary to make one aware of this truth.

Thus the problems involved are: how to find the key, and how to produce tones smoothly graded in intensity.

Two factors produce a need for an in-and-out adjustment while horizontal distance is being manipulated: the shortness of the thumb, and the difference in the distance from the body of the white and black keys.

The easy covering of this distance is an adjustment to it by top arm and forearm, which produces a sort of scallop in movement. If this distance is made a part of the responsibility of fingers and thumb there will be a definite increase in the difficulty of playing arpeggios. If you do not believe the top arm and forearm quite naturally and easily can make this adjustment and add to the fluency and ease and beauty in arpeggio playing, all that is needed to prove it is to see *and hear* a talented eight-year-old play fluent and beautiful arpeggios. A gifted child playing naturally—without interference from teaching—is a wonderful example of what can be used in a blended activity to make playing easy. Supposedly nothing in his equipment, physically, is adequate; hand is too small and muscles are not developed. Yet he plays and with complete ease and charm. But he certainly does not play arpeggios with a key legato and with an inactive top arm and forearm.

The top arm moves in and out, and the forearm, with hand, has an exaggerated alternating action.

This is the solution of easy arpeggio playing. If top arm and forearm are the dominating actions for covering distance, they will also have the chance of being involved with tone production. The hand and fingers extend this action of the powerful levers. It is then that arpeggios lose their difficulty.

It is a self-evident fact that by hook or crook arpeggios must lose their preliminary difficulty or they cannot be played with either facility or accuracy. In observing arpeggios easily played, be sure to watch the top arm and alternating action. *See* if they are not in constant operation, whether the resulting scallop be tiny or large. The larger the hand, the less the need for exaggerated activity elsewhere for covering the distance. If the hand easily covers a tenth, there is less need for adaptation along the arm than if the hand barely spans an octave.

The solution of smooth brilliant arpeggios hinges on the activity of the top arm, and this activity is very much the same for arpeggios as for the glissando. Only every sort of complication is put in the way of its being the same. For the glissando the top arm furnishes a direct control for horizontal distance and power for tone, without any interference from forearm, hand or fingers. Quite automatically these other levers *conform* as a simple extension of the top arm pull: they offer no individual actions.

It is this conforming to a central control that is destroyed by training fingers as independent digits. It is this conforming to a central control that produces the astonishing virtuosity of the gifted child. If the gifted child is not available, hunt out an untaught gifted jazz player who plays by ear. He also will astonish and delight with his easy arpeggios.

The differences in playing the glissando and arpeggios are multiple; yet there must be the same basic relationship of top arm to the other levers. The top arm furnishes the central control for in-and-out distance and horizontal distance. Also it maintains the same gauging of level for tone production that it does for the glissando—this is very important.

For the glissando there is no question about this relationship of the top arm to the level where tone is produced. If the fingers, hand or forearm have any bearing down on their own initiative, the glissando simply does not come off. They each become an integrated unit with the top arm control; they make the top arm effective in contacting tone.

A very realistic and vivid sensation of the top arm control of the glissando is an excellent starting point for the understanding of the cooperation which can be given by forearm, hand and fingers. Cooperation and not independence of action can also be given by these same levers in arpeggio playing, if the *timing* of their actions in arpeggio playing is used to extend and augment the primary control in the top arm.

But *cooperation, not independence in action, by hand, fingers and forearm must be what is practiced—not individual controls* —if cooperation is believed in and desired, and is to be the *result* of *practice*. It is exactly this point which is basically unsound, in my opinion, in traditional training. Tradition believes in training levers for independent actions. The result is simply independent action—not cooperative actions. That is not nature's way of creating an expert coordination.

Again think of the expert playing of the talented eight-year-old. By what process did this expertness take form? Not by eight hours a day of practicing finger exercises over a period of years. There was no period of years. It happened by the very simple process of the child's finding the tones on the keyboard which fitted the aural pattern dictated by imaged sounds. Nature made all the movements that were necessary for the desired result. The child no more knew what these movements were than if he were reaching for a piece of candy which he *saw* on a plate. No one thinks of paying attention to the movements made in getting food into the mouth or achieving any of the desired results in daily living. Yet the movements involved certainly become expert with repetition.

A *desired result* produces an expert coordination—that is nature's way of giving us what we want.

The principle is exactly the same for expert piano playing, even though the process is highly complex; the ear asks for a desired result and the body performs to achieve it. It is the fact that we have bungled by making more complex an already complex procedure that has caused innumerable failures instead of successes in having fun with playing.

Plenty of people, of course, do not have the necessary ear control to help facilitate the learning of a musical skill. A talent for playing does have this ear control, and it should be helped to function naturally—not hindered by tearing a natural unified control into shreds through independent motivations.

This will mean that, in response to the aural image, the top arm starts the activity for finding the key. Its initiative quite automatically brings the forearm, hand and fingers into their functioning position. If with its initiation for finding the key it maintains control of the lever for tone in arpeggio playing, as it does for the glissando, there is produced a central control which can develop an expert coordination for the arm as a whole.

The finding of the key comes first.

The lever and the pull bring the power for tone into action. The finding of the key operates with the pull and it is this important factor in tone production, the pull, that differs so greatly, when there is articulation for key-drop, from the glissando. With articulation two things immediately happen: there is a vertical action not controlled by the top arm, and there is the possibility of emphasis with the playing of a single tone. Where the glissando is concerned, everything is controlled by the one horizontal pull. Now, in arpeggios, the situation is much more complicated; but if that horizontal control disappears when definite articulative actions come into the picture, with it will disappear the physical action which is the counterpart of the musical idea as a whole. Instead of one continuous sweep of power to the close of the phrase, there will be only separate key actions—a note-wise production which breeds note-wise listening. Then the coordination for handling dynamics with the utmost subtlety gets bogged down.

This vertical key control must be an action timed and coordinated with the control for horizontal progression if piano playing is produced with a basic rhythm and any continuity in the power for tone. Without these two factors, piano playing is helpless in its competition with other instruments for sensitive grace in phrase modeling.

The glissando, which does nothing but use the horizontal pull, can help enormously in achieving an integration of this pull with the actions of articulation—vertical actions. Keep its sensation in the body while reading the analysis which involves the timing of all levers with this central control.

The pull for arpeggios changes from that of the glissando in two definite aspects: direction and evenness in the rate of progression. The glissando uses only white *or* black keys. It does not use both at the same time. Arpeggios use both, and the manner in which the keys are contacted poses the problem to be solved. This problem deals with every lever in the playing mechanism. The top arm must be related to tone production if a full coordination of the arm is realized. This can easily happen if it initiates the control for in-and-out and horizontal distance; and if it initiates and maintains the gauging of the level where energy for tone is to be released.

Frequently in teaching I close the lid over the keys and have the pupil rest the elbows on the lid. Then, in this position, initiate a tiny back and forth movement with the top arm, sufficient to shake the hand. Be very sure that it is top arm and not forearm activity which shakes the hand. It need be only a tiny movement, and the position on the lid need not be shifted.

The actual contact with this positive level and activity against this resistance make for a vivid realization of what is needed in the controls of the top arm in its normal relationship to the keyboard.

Observe the initiation of control of the in-and-out distance by the top arm when playing chromatic octaves. Here is a completely natural activity with the top arm in relation to in-and-out distance. You can imagine that the point of the elbow draws an unbroken line over each successive key from the beginning to the end of the chromatic scale. This same in-and-out pattern by the top arm is to be seen in the case of arpeggios, as stated before, as a sort of scallop.

The indentation (the "in") is with the thumb; the convexity is with the fingers. Two, three or four fingers may be used between thumb actions, so the scallop may vary in the time between thumb actions as well as in the distance between the keys. Since the control of horizontal progression is related to the placement of the hand as it is passed, the rate of progression will vary with the distance and time between thumb actions. The important issue is not the rate of progression, but is in *consistent* progression even though the rate of speed varies. *Activity in the top arm does not stop in its relation to controlling distance.* No matter what activity in forearm, hand and fingers supplements its action, top arm remains the arbiter of distance and level, and it produces some of the power for successive tones.

Acting as a fulcrum for the forearm need never destroy the top arm's control of level and distance. It can move slightly to initiate the control of distance *while* it acts as a fulcrum for the forearm. The initiation of a control demands no large movement. It means simply that the top arm assumes the primary response to the aural image. Any or all of the other levers follow through to supplement the primary action.

The point is that unless the control starts at the center of the radius of activity for playing, there cannot be a fused and subtly timed action by all the levers involved. If separated controls produce tones, they will annihilate a completely coordinated equipment. In this event a basic rhythm is not used for making the music delightful, and neither is full power for tone production consistently on tap. And then arpeggios are never a fluent means of making music.

Note that in the controls for distance which form the scallop, there is always a fusion of the in-and-out and horizontal distances. Neither the in-and-out nor the horizontal lines are straight. They both operate as shallow curves.

From shoulder joint to finger there is a shortening and lengthening process of the arm in constant operation. It is somewhat like a carriage on an office telephone. It shuts up or lengthens out. The shortening process of the arm operates while the fingers are being used, and the lengthening while the thumb is being used. Remember, though, that no such process in the human machinery is cut and dried, and distinct one from the other. There is always a dovetailing and overlapping.

The factors for real concern in arpeggio playing are:

1. That the hand is thrown into position—the action which takes place at the wrist in the passing operation is the *result* of an action farther back in the arm. It is not a locally controlled action.

2. That *while* the hand is being thrown into a new position (moved horizontally on the keyboard), the top arm is on its way to finding the key and is maintaining the control of the level at which tone is produced.

Clarify these two actions and any real resistance to easy arpeggios will have been broken down.

First of all, the hand cannot be thrown if a key-connection legato is believed in and practiced. The operation for throwing the hand sidewise in both directions is, of course, opposite. Illustrating with the right hand, when it is thrown to the right the untwist of the rotary action is so easily available with a quick extension of the forearm that the slight pull of the top arm toward the torso is hardly noticed. When the hand is thrown to the left (remember the playing stance has used up practically all the twist of rotary), there is very little available twist of rotary to be used with quick flexion of the forearm, so the top arm swing away from the torso is more in evidence.

The top arm movement, tiny or otherwise, starts the entire action. It is always the action which makes the forearm able to act efficiently for piano playing.

The forearm movement is always conspicuous because it operates in a wider arc of distance than does the top arm. But ignore the top arm as the *primary* control and the blended action of arm which has such enormous efficiency is damaged to the point of destroying real virtuosity.

So remember the glissando. Play ripped chords and watch the operation of the top arm. It pulls and turns in the socket at the same time. It is a pull that furnishes its action as fulcrum when it must be steady to make the forearm effective in action. It is a pull when it takes key-drop for important tones. Like the control of the lariat, it is a pull that insistently gauges the level where tone is produced.

Exchange the word pull for draw if it assists in making the sensation of top arm activity clear. One *draws* a circle. The drawing is not manipulated with a hinge joint alone.

The top arm moves in and out and around and about. Each of these movements is a segment of a circle. Draw it with the tip of the elbow. If thinking the action at the tip of the elbow helps to vivify the activity which takes place at the shoulder joint, which moves the top arm in relation to its initiating the control for all distance and level—by all means use the sensation of drawing parts of a circle for the activity of the top arm.

The problem for the pianist is to succeed in feeling that the action of the top arm, which not only taps the greatest reservoir of power but at the same time possesses the tremendous asset of continuity in action, is as much involved with the beauty of the pianist's phrase as is the breath supply for the singer. This is no problem at all if his learning has been achieved through a fundamental rhythm, but it is a difficult problem if the learning has taken place with isolated actions of articulation.

The arpeggio must feel like the glissando in spite of the functioning of the forearm and hand for springing the little trap door—the key-drop. The chord formation of the arpeggio is taken in the palm exactly as is the span of the octave. The fingers are an extension of this action.

Localize this sensation by abducting the thumb with its palm segment and opening the hand knuckles, while holding a slightly closed fist. Then extend the fingers and thumb into the chord pattern. Arpeggios are simply a series of opened chords: do not relax the feeling of the chord in the palm between successive formations.

These opened chords should possess the same relationship to the top arm control that a ripped chord does. With the ripped chord there is a dominating action with the top arm and practically no awareness that there is finger action at all. In other words, there is continuity in the central power which is implemented by the fingers. I call that the *horizontal control.* There is a strong horizontal action in the ripped chord—activity back of articulation. It is this horizontal, key-finding, level-controlling, power-producing action of the top arm for the ripped chord which should be carried over into arpeggio playing. It should furnish the activity between tones.

If the time space between tones is filled in by the movements of articulation it will mean that those actions are seeking key position. Then the important control for distance gets into the periphery. Note-wise progression and note-wise listening result, and all the subtlety in handling dynamics disappears along with a basic rhythm.

When the movements of articulation are actively involved in finding the key, they are never idle. They should be idle until the power comes along. Articulation should take place only when the central power crosses the beam of the little trap door —the key-drop—like those gates which open when you come into a certain relation with the "electric eye" which springs them open.

If there is success in slowing down the ripped chord without the fingers increasing their activity—not an easy thing to do— all the right controls for arpeggios will be in operation: the central power has access to all the fingers and it fills in the time space between tones. For actually playing the arpeggio, this central power, plus alternating action and rotary, places the hand in its successive positions along the keyboard, as already described.

Faulty manipulation of distance can completely balk arpeggios. So can a faulty control of "direction." Direction can be related to the turn of the arpeggio if it goes up and comes back without stopping; or to an arpeggio which has backward jogs in its long ascending and descending line. Both of these factors are present in the example from the Chopin Etude, Op. 25, No. 11 (Illustration 11, page 119). It is an excellent arpeggio for realizing just how different playing can be made by faulty and right controls. This pattern never becomes really easy so long as a key legato and reaching for position with fingers are practiced. It loses all its difficulty when there is no pretense at legato playing and the control for distance is given to the top arm.

Three chordal positions are involved, and with each there are keys to be played which lie below the ascending line—backward jogs in the long line up the keyboard. If these jogs in an opposite direction are not taken by a variety of levers *without* a switch in direction by the top arm, progression in the long line is definitely hampered, and that will mean difficulty in being accurate. This is easily understood, but the fact remains that this shift in direction remains a difficult thing to diagnose and is very frequently the primary cause of insecurity and difficulty. A long sweep in movement is much easier than an action which involves switches in that sweep.

If the tones were played as actual chords there would be no turning back; yet all the tones would be sounded. As chords, *all five fingers* very naturally stand under *one* power. They do the same thing for the ripped chord. One dominant action by the top arm activates the tones and the fingers transmit this action to the keys. The fingers are completely adequate in this role. So is the top arm power. It is the relationship between fingers and the powerful lever which causes no strain. This relationship can be maintained in arpeggios, and as a matter of fact it is maintained by the player who achieves great velocity and clarity—no matter what he thinks or says, he does.

But this relationship cannot be maintained if one believes in a key-connection legato. In order to maintain the relationship between fingers and one dominant power, so naturally accomplished in a ripped chord, passing must be an affair of the hand as a unit. This can only be achieved with expertness, when the hand is thrown, propelled, into position by the top arm, plus forearm and rotary. In other words, the hand is conducted along the keyboard.

This throwing of the hand involves a break in key connection. It *need not* involve a break in the even flow of dynamics, which is the all-important factor. It *will not* involve a break in dynamics if the top arm produces a canopy of power over all five fingers all the time; and the fingers simply furnish a structure to support that canopy.

This is the solution to easy, fluent, brilliant arpeggios. A key legato in passing destroys this highly advantageous relationship of fingers to power, or power to fingers.

In one instance—no key legato and the hand placed as a unit —the thumb is simply the first digit of a chord ripped slowly and evenly. In the other instance—a key legato in passing—the thumb finds its own key, and *after* it has played the hand assumes the position necessary for the easy functioning of the other fingers. This latter situation is simply too clumsy for any gifted player to tolerate, so he quite naturally discards it if he ever used it in a slow tempo under orders.

This legato in passing is a pertinent example of teaching which establishes a habit in a slow tempo which cannot be used expertly for speed. The result is that the gifted player will not use it for speed, but the less gifted will not find the way out and will always be hampered by a habit which does not foster speed.

The power of the top arm can very easily be available to all the fingers when the hand is passed as a unit. All that is demanded is that its rate of progression be determined by this availability. It must not move too fast to cover a finger which plays below the long line of direction. At the exact moment of tone production, articulation should mean that it has completed the contact of the arm power with the key level for tone. *It should never mean that movements of articulation become disconnected from the arm power.*

Frequently the turn of the arpeggio from going up to coming down the keyboard causes trouble for no reason except that the power kept on going up to the very last key before the turn took place. The moment the last chordal position is taken by the hand the power (top arm control) *need* go no farther and *must* not go farther. It can cover all five fingers from the last thumb position and during the playing of this last chordal position the change in direction is made to conform to all the opposite controls for passing the hand down the keyboard.

The turning of the humerus in the shoulder joint is always so smooth and natural and easy that it is almost imperceptible, and therefore easily ignored if faulty habits have diminished its full usefulness. But unless the top arm does initiate the control for direction—always a part of the control for finding the key— the entire blended activity for playing will lose its perfection in balance, the very nucleus of virtuosity with arpeggios.

Every ounce of awareness of the complete association in activity of the top arm with all the other movements of the forearm and hand will pay dividends in piano playing. Observe it when washing your hands and when rubbing in a hand lotion. Every movement made in these operations is made also in piano playing, especially in passing the hand. Don't just think this action. Put some hand lotion in your palm and then spread it over the entire hand (backs and palm) and watch the top arm steer those movements.

The *problems* posed in arpeggio playing are:

1. To find the key without a positive control of reaching for it with fingers; control of distance is at the center, not at the periphery of the playing mechanism.

2. To achieve articulation on the way to a rhythmic goal: the antithesis of a note-wise procedure.

The *solutions* are:

A. 1. To use the top arm for gauging all distance.

2. To use, with the key-finding action, the top arm for continuity in action in the playing mechanism: the action which initiates the basic rhythm.

3. To use the top arm for gauging the level at which power is released for tone production.

4. To use the top arm for taking the key-drop and producing the power for important tones.

5. To use the top arm as fulcrum for the activity of the forearm and, in this role, to share in the power for all tones.

6. To have top arm activity *the initial activity between tones*—activity for articulation should take place only at the second of tone production and *should not continue to press against the keybed.*

B. 1. To use the forearm, which includes rotary action, for propelling the hand into position for the chordal sequences.

2. To use the forearm to initiate the control of the vertical key action, except when top arm takes the key-drop, and for sharing the production of power for tone.

3. To use the rotary action for sharing key-drop and horizontal distance, as well as power for tone.

C. 1. To use the hand as the *completion,* the *extension* of the action of top arm and forearm for all distance and power, not as an independent tool of action.

2. To use the hand to maintain a chord formation, a control which takes place in the palm between hand knuckle joint of little finger and second joint of the thumb—never at the tips of fingers.

D. 1. To use the fingers as a bony structure to stand under the arm power—never to produce power on their own, independently of the power of the arm.

2. To use the fingers for *sharing* the vertical distance of key-drop, with all the leverage of the arm, including the hand.

3. To think of finger action as the last link completing the bony structure between the shoulder and keybed. The *bony structure* of fingers is *completely adequate* for transmitting the power of the arms to the key. The *muscle power* of the fingers is *totally inadequate* for producing a full range of dynamics.

First, last and forever, if you would avoid a note-wise procedure, there must be a physical action in the playing mechanism which proceeds from the first tone of the phrase to the last tone—such as the glissando insures. This action may go directly from one accent to another and use these accents as stepping stones in its procedure to the close of the musical statement. *This is always the action produced with the top arm*: that is the fact to be kept vividly in mind. It is what matters most if one wishes to play with facility and beauty, for this action, coupled with activity in the torso, produces the rhythm of the phrase, and it taps the greatest reserves of power. It also produces the most subtle control for the use of dynamics.

As has been noted before, to say that an action must be thus or so in relation to a musical pattern is a hazardous thing to do. Tempo, emotion, and the desire for brilliance may alter the production; but the following concrete analysis of an arpeggio pattern can be used for velocity and brilliance, and that is the proof that it is based on a sound principle.

With fingers reaching for position and producing power for tone, with a key legato as part of the picture, this arpeggio balked me for six years. With practically no work at all it became a very easy pattern when I used the relationship about to be set down:

III. 11

Note that the chordal position uses four tones, but that the meter uses groups of six tones.

The scallop—the direct, continuous physical action of the top arm which is related to the musical idea and not to individual tones—uses the six-tone grouping as its nucleus for procedure. Play a glissando using a scallop instead of a straight line. It will give a clear sensation of the activity of the top arm in the arpeggio, and note its gauging of the level where tone is produced. The scallop quite naturally will relate itself to the in-and-out distance needed for the tones which are to be produced as it travels toward its destination. Whether or not the top arm actually takes the key-drop at the beginning of each scallop in a performance when there is full steam on to present the musical idea, it will do no damage to use it thus in the detailed analysis which follows.

There is danger of being influenced by the *appearance* of the scallop as illustrated. Get the *sensation* of activity—the aware-

ness of how tiny a movement of top arm can be and yet be
related to movement by other levers—by action when the elbow
maintains contact with the closed lid over the keys. The top
arm acts in a tiny orbit. It is the forearm and hand which cover
most of the horizontal distance; and, of course, all horizontal
distance is facilitated quite naturally by movement of the torso.

The following detailed analysis of action involved in articulating each tone can give no conception of the subtle blending
and dovetailing of all the movements. Only a going rhythm can
produce that result; so cling to the sensation of the top arm
scallop.

5   Any first tone is produced by a full arm stroke; the whole
A   mechanism is brought in contact with tone.

2   E involves only the vertical distance of key-drop. Flexion
E   of forearm plus flexion of hand (the latter is a downward
    movement which can only take place in relation to flexion
    of forearm in piano playing), plus a very slight twist of rotary
    plus flexion of finger at hand knuckle.

4   The same continued flexion of forearm and hand is used for
G   G, plus untwist of rotary and finger flexion.

1   The playing of B♭ is synchronized with the placing of the
B♭ hand for the new chordal position. The actions are a quick
    extension of forearm which throws the hand into its new
    position, and at the same time shares the distance of key-
    drop, plus the twist of rotary and thumb abduction—down-
    ward movement. None of this synchronized action can take
    place if key legato is believed in and practiced. It has to
    happen if there is to be no difficulty with this distance:
    horizontal, in-and-out, and vertical. Chord formation in the
    palm should be maintained while this passing operation
    takes place.

5 Again flexion of forearm and hand (it will continue for E
A and G), plus untwist of rotary action and finger action.

2 The same as A, except rotary action is slight twist.
E

4 Top arm takes initiative for key-drop, plus flexion of forearm
G and hand, with untwist of rotary plus finger action.

The tones of the first three scallops are produced in a like
manner; and then with the next scallop there is a change of
direction to going down the keyboard. This change is barely
perceptible until the passing from B♭ to A takes place; but
there is a change in the aim of the top arm. It prepares in advance to facilitate the passing by a slight swing away from the
torso. This action is made to produce the right plane for action
of the forearm in placing the hand.

The arpeggio down uses the same blended activity but with
some of the movements in reverse direction. There is the same
scallop with the top arm, but the turn of the humerus is in the
opposite direction.

5 2 4 The same flexion of forearm and hand fused with the
AE♭G pull, or draw, of the top arm operates while the fingers
       connect up with A, E♭ and G. The main direction of
       rotary is toward the thumb, but there is a miniature un-
       twist for G.

1 B♭ is produced with extension of forearm and hand, with
B♭ all possible remaining twist of rotary plus thumb action.

5 This passing from B♭ to A, from 1 to 5 finger, means a
A very quick shift of the hand horizontally. It is achieved
   by a turn of the humerus which swings the elbow out
   and up, plus a flexion of forearm which throws the hand

laterally and down at the same time. The key-drop is taken by flexion of the hand with untwist of rotary plus finger. The untwist of rotary plus the chord formation in the palm places the hand in an advantageous position for the following tones. This can only be accomplished if key legato is not a part of the picture.

2
Eb

Eb takes the same flexion as A, with twist of rotary plus finger action.

4
G

G begins another scallop. Top arm can take part of the distance of the key-drop, with the same continued flexion of forearm and hand (started with A) plus a slight untwist of rotary and finger.

The salient points to remember are:

1. The top arm produces the only continuous action. It is active between tones and regulates their spacing in response to the aural image.
2. Movements of articulation are not legato. They are *idle* between tones. They do *not* maintain pressure against keybed between tones. They do *not* prepare in advance. They simply connect up with the power of the top arm at the exact instant when tone is demanded.
3. The smoothness in dynamics in passing is dependent on the continuity of the top arm in maintaining progression and level for tone, and in covering both of the fingers involved when passing takes place.
4. The rhythm of the musical idea is dependent upon this continuity of action in the top arm, and always it is a basic rhythm which provides the element necessary for a complete synchronization of all the factors involved.
5. Keep in mind the destination and level and sweep of action of the glissando.

SCALES

Scales which are of the essence of beautiful playing can develop habits which will prevent beautiful playing if they are practiced too soon. They should never, never be used as the basis for developing a technique.

The reasons seem obvious to me. All virtuosity and brilliance demand a blended, synchronized use of the total equipment of the performer. To achieve that synchronization, one does not go about developing habits which are opposed to it. Practice perfects only the movements in use.

Scales—a diatonic progression—would foster the use of fingers even if traditional teaching did not emphasize their use in scale playing. Fingers, as stated here repeatedly, are only the periphery of the total mechanism. Emphasis on their use does not develop a blended action of all the levers needed for fluent playing.

Scales practiced with a finger technique establish habits which are diametrically opposed to the habits which foster virtuosity and brilliance. But scales which use an *established* blended activity can refine that activity to its *n*th degree and increase the beauty of the performer's output.

Scales should use *exactly* the same production as arpeggios. There is no difference between them as far as the need of a blended activity goes. But the diatonic progression does not show up that need as do arpeggios. Thus, unless the blended activity of the whole mechanism has already become the natural manner of playing, scales will emphasize action at periphery, to the detriment of the activity which is the complement of a basic rhythm.

The answer to every question, every argument, is which solution uses a basic rhythm. There is no other reason of equal importance for making a decision.

A note-wise procedure in scale playing will prevent the use of the scale as an intrinsic musical pattern of great beauty. But the scale produced by the follow-through action of the top arm, with all the other levers assisting, cooperating with that rhythmic follow-through, can make one shiver with delight.

The articulation in the scale connects up with the arm power as it comes along, just as it does in the glissando.

Think of that simple mechanism and know that even with all the complications of articulation the top arm maintains its relationship to destination and level; and in so doing allows the basic rhythm to reign supreme in scale playing. Let the scale be the result of an established coordination. Let it just be a beautiful idea and use it simply as music for a long time before an attempt is made to refine all the movements to the point of achieving perfection.

Let the other forms establish the necessary blended activity for playing. Then perfect the scale.

Learning with a Rhythm

Now is the time to believe in magic.

To experience the transformation which can take place when a rhythm holds and sways the music (instead of letting the habits, which are the result of routine drill and note-wise listening, tie the music down) is to know that here is an element which disregards almost everything we have believed in and substitutes a luminous insight which we never knew we possessed.

This rhythm is far more expert than the most expert coach in relating tones and phrases in a manner which graces musical speech. It *is* that grace by its physical activity; and not to feel it and play with it is to have missed the most exhilarating, stimulating and satisfying experience in making music.

It would be difficult to believe (it is difficult to believe, even so) that a simple physical activity can accomplish what no amount of knowledge and detailed practice have accomplished in producing music with that breathtaking charm, were it not for the fact that it is infallible. It works every time—not once in ten, but every time.

Rhythm always has the last word in the argument as to which way the phrase should be turned. The solutions in difficult Beethoven passages cannot be found without it. Rhythm is the simplest and by far the most efficient of all tools for getting results. Probably it is the amazing simplicity of its operation which has made it difficult to find and believe in.

Somewhere, staunchly embedded in the unconscious, our faith lies in the complicated, hard-to-achieve approach. We don't believe in the easy way. But the more magnificent the equipment of the artist, both musically and technically, the simpler the music sounds and the easier the playing looks; and there is no such artist who is not endowed with a superlative rhythmic sense. So perhaps it was just his great good fortune which saved the day. This rhythm never got choked out while he practiced his scales, but instead it flourished and grew and always commanded the situation. The scales might have been the conscious effort, but it was the unconscious natural rhythm which really implemented the results.

I know of no complicated procedure for utilizing the magic of this rhythm. Meter, form and technique are not only more easily learned when the cue to their problems is a rhythm, but they are more efficiently learned: a greater awareness of subtleties in tonal relationships is developed when they are handled as a rhythmic unit.

There is no boredom when learning with a rhythm. The learning process is full of surprises and exciting experiences. It is also so easy to achieve; simply by creating activity in the area of top arm and torso, the entire body responds to the mood of the music. Is it gay—is it sad—is it a dance—or is it of the essence of a dream: the activity of the body with its follow-through will create the kind of activity which expresses the emotional response to the music—*if* the emotional surge stimulates its being. Learning can see to it that the emotional excitement is the cause of the complete bodily activity.

Put music in the ears, music which causes the pulses to quicken, and then let the playing mechanism and the body express it. Think of the rhythmic expressions of primitive peoples. Lose the inhibitions you may have felt necessary to prevent exaggeration in movements which have been labeled mannerisms. Don't think about mannerisms. *Feel* the music with every fibre of your being and then know that to express every jot of that feeling the entire body must be involved. That can mean only one thing—that the initiation of power (top arm) plus its fulcrum (torso) pick up the emotional response to the music.

The suggestions made for learning with a rhythm could not possibly be exhaustive. They are simply a few of the definite means which have been successfully used. They have never failed to produce exciting results: and that is a sober statement of fact.

Since the manner in which a meter is learned can assist or corrupt a rhythm, it is a very important matter. "Learning to count" can be a bitter period for a beginner, for it is often an obstruction to an accomplished experience in playing.

An integral factor in a rhythm is that it is going forward: its essence is destination. It is possessed of a follow-through. It never stands still. It creates relationships by this going forward to a destination.

Meter is a detail of rhythm. It must be of the same fibre if it is to help produce cohesion and beauty in the completed idea. That means that meter must have the same innate quality of going forward which belongs to a rhythm. Learning meter by counting has a way of relating tones to what has preceded instead of to what is to follow. It deals with addition more than it deals with division.

No pain is too great to avoid this state of affairs, for there is no possibility of the ultimate in refinement of spacing tones, of taking care of details, except as they fill an established unit of time. This means a dividing up of that unit of time—not an adding up of one tone after another to what has gone before, but a fulfilling, a going forward to a completed statement.

Moving ahead by a relationship backward is almost a natural result of learning meter by counting aloud. But learning meter by the process of subdividing a time unit quite naturally relates it forward, and thus it not only fits into the swinging balance of a long line rhythm, but its learning has fostered the very attributes of that rhythm. Especially is this true when the time units—the rims of the pattern—are felt with the whole body initiating distance; and nothing could be simpler than that accomplishment. It was in this process of rocking in the rim tones of the pattern (Illustration 12) that a pupil said, "I never felt a rhythm until I felt the swaying of my body."

These patterns that I shall discuss are more than efficient; they have a quality of revealing tonal relationships as well as producing time values.

Illustration 12 shows the use of rhythm for a time unit subdivided into halves, quarters, and thirds.

Ill. 12   *Pattern 1*

etc.

Pattern 2

etc.

Pattern 3

etc.

Pattern 4

etc.

Pattern 5

etc.

Pattern 6

etc.

Pattern 7

etc.

Pattern 8

"Rock" in the outside tones, the rim tones. That is, let the sidewise swing of the torso bring the hand in contact with the keybed—ignore all activity except the swing of the torso. When the sound of the rim tones is synchronized with the rock of the torso, then is the time to fill in the tones which lie between the outside tones (white keys only used). For the idea of equalized spacing of the filled tones, all that is needed is a good example produced by the teacher. Let this happen incidentally while the regularity of the rim tones is being established.

The relationship between a dotted note and a short note can be easily and efficiently realized by not sounding D and E, and the result of relating F to G will be established (Patterns 4 and 5). All too frequently, because the short note is attached to the dotted note as we look at it, there is a failure to relate the short note forward as it is played.

If a child is learning this relationship of the dotted note to the short note, no explanation of mathematics is necessary. The hearing and feeling are sufficient for the time being.

The right result in playing is the desirable achievement—not the intellectual process first. That can wait a bit.

The crucial point for effective use of the patterns is to keep the rim tones going. Shift from right to left hand; change the inside of the pattern—but never stop the rim tones. Establish an inevitability in the swaying and playing of the outside tones. They should go on and on until regularity is a positive and well-established fact. Only then can the relationships in filling in the pattern, either even or uneven, become pertinent.

Herein lies the secret of easy manipulation of two against three, and three against four, and all complications of meter. *Both* hands play the rim tones *always*. But only one hand fills at a time, until the aural image of the tones filled in is so strong, so vivid, that it can easily direct both hands at the same time.

Any complication in meter must be *heard* and *felt*. Meters pitted against each other will always remain difficult otherwise. It isn't mathematics that solves the problem. It is the aural image plus its physical counterpart—a progression toward a goal—that establishes the solution.

Much more playing of the rim tones than filling in speeds up the desired result. Pupils are prone to do the reverse: once the rims have been filled, to keep on filling. It should be the other way round: rims always and many times alone, with filling in only now and then.

The scale which we are conditioned to finishing by constant hearings can be used as an extension of these patterns. We have the rim tones as "do" and what lies between completes a musical idea.

The realization that this already conditioned pattern could be utilized for feeling a cohesion in form was the starting point for using any and all such available musical ideas, and superimposing their *feeling* of continuity to the close upon fresh material which did not possess that strong feeling of completing the musical idea. Folk tunes or popular songs furnish a wealth of such material. No one will stop in the middle of a word or phrase when humming "Old Black Joe" or "Ol' Man River." The words are meaningful and the music fits the words: both make sense only when they are completed. Using this feeling of necessity to follow through, using the physical action which is the counterpart of the musical form, for creating a like rhythmic continuity in relation to new material, has proven to be a fascinating and productive means of developing a sense of form. It has limitless possibilities—this transferring of a sensation from an old context to a new one.

Here is a method of procedure which is largely unexplored and undeveloped and unused for assistance in projecting an idea; and it is vastly more expert in producing the desired results than editors' marks or coaching.

Any procedure which uses the physical attributes of a going rhythm in learning is a creative force which develops potential ability. In trying out Pattern 4, the transfer of the scale as a musical unit to the Chopin Prelude, Op. 28, No. 7 (Illustration 13) should be absorbed only in the physical sensation of the

Ill. 13

scale. Sense the attribute in action which proceeds from "do" to "do." If it is not sufficiently vivid, play a number of glissando scales where the horizontal progression completely dominates the operation. It is this horizontal action, the feeling of progression along the keyboard, which produces the feeling of form. It is this particular sensation which is to be used in the transfer from scale to Prelude. Play glissando scales and then dash off a scale using finger articulation, and see if the control of horizontal progression remains intact.

The C-major scale is used purposely for two reasons: it makes the glissando available for pointing up the sensation of horizontal progression, and the disassociation from the key of the

Prelude may help to isolate the physical sensation—make it more dominant for the moment than the ears. It is the physical sensation that is being transferred: it must be as vivid as possible.

Constantly using C major for the simple patterns and the scale, instead of the key of the composition, helps in detaching the attention from listening and allowing greater attention on the physical attributes of musical progression.

Tempo is not too important in the first stages of making the transfer; it is not so important as the feeling of going toward a destination. Without the feeling of destination there is no emphasis on the scale as a musical idea. If the tempo is slowed down to conform to the tempo of the Prelude, it allows the ears to usurp too great a control at this moment of trying for a physical sensation. At least avoid losing the sensation of the progression of the scale.

Learning with a rhythm means constantly increasing the awareness of the physical activity in the fulcrums: torso and top arm. The dominance of this activity in the scale playing is the coveted attribute at the moment. Shut out the ear distractions as much as possible in order to feel the rhythm as much as possible. Once the spacing of the tones of the scale on their way to a finished statement has become related to the first chord of each measure of the phrase of the Prelude, with an identical feeling of progression, then a realistic, right tempo can be established without damage. The filling in process must not be allowed to dissipate the established feeling that the first beats are consecutive and progress to the close of the phrase— just as simply and directly as the scale was played from "do" to "do." *Never start the filling in process at the beginning of the phrase. First establish a strong feeling of going forward to the close of the statement.* Then when the body feels the rhythmic urge to complete the musical idea, as a counterpart of the aural image, slip in a third beat now and then. Slip these beats in and out, but always without damaging the simple procedure related to consecutive first beats. Unless there is success in maintaining that simple procedure, there has not been success in filling in—tucking tones in on the way. Rather, the horizontal progression has been disturbed by putting in some details.

Arriving at as definite a feeling of progression with this eight-measure phrase as was had with the simple scale will illuminate its form in a penetrating manner. It leaves no fuzziness in feeling form. It makes for a musical speech which adds both subtlety and grace to its inflection.

The scale comes first as a concrete experience in transferring a sensation from one context to another. Then comes the realization that every successfully played phrase could be used in just the same manner. All that is needed is to find the successful phrase. It will be a phrase which lilts because it has made a strong appeal. Pick out the tunes which make the strongest rhythmic appeal. Play them with emotion. Then superimpose the feeling, the same lilt, on to an unsuccessful or an unlearned composition. Popular tunes, lazy waltzes, and smooth, going, rhythmic playing: the essence of their grace can be used in other contexts.

Along with using this method of transferring sensation, use improvisation. If there is insufficient talent to improvise a tune with its harmonies, use rhythmic patterns with a repeated tone. Improvising cannot start unless some idea is formulated. The fact that an idea takes place will mean a going forward to its conclusion. It is this starting with a definite purpose of fulfilling, completing the idea, which produces action that does not sag and fall apart. It is like the stride of a person bent on getting to a destination—not like the person loafing in the park.

The talented person who loves to improvise and does it expertly does not necessarily play the classics with the same kind of delightful rhythmic flow. The improvising uses ears and rhythm as a fused unit. The eye, reading, or habits of practice can and frequently do interfere with this fusion of ear and rhythm, and the result in playing is a lack of rhythmic progression which distorts dynamics and creates a performance without any of the charm which was a part of the improvising.

For these same talented people, a conscious use of the sensation of the rhythmic follow-through in their improvising can be productive, for all their other playing, of startlingly better results.

Each person will use the means which work most easily and efficiently. It is the result and not the means that matters. To capture that feeling of rhythmic grace and hold onto it and use it in learning the literature of the piano makes for an approach in learning which not only does away with unmusical practice but creates amazing results in beauty and facility. Technical problems will succumb when a simple rhythmic pattern is superimposed upon them—problems that hours of routine drill cannot dislodge.

For instance, the simple chromatic octave pattern (Illustration 10, page 100) has produced excellent results. Obviously the pattern itself must feel smooth and easy and graceful if its sensation is made valuable for transferring. The horizontal progression must feel as smooth as a glissando and as continuous in the application of power from the top arm.

Here is a simple review of the attributes of a rhythm:

1. A basic rhythm stems from top arm plus its fulcrum (torso).
2. It has its continuity in action in fulcrums—top arm and torso.
3. The top arm is the dominating lever in the playing mechanism for gauging distance and for the application of power to the key.
4. A rhythm means a follow-through in the playing mechanism.
5. A rhythm proceeds by important tones—never note-wise. Tones get tucked in on the way to a destination.
6. Tucking in always involves the use of any or all the other levers, while the top arm plus torso is creating a rhythmic continuity.

The simple chromatic octave pattern highlights these attributes when it feels as smooth as velvet. Feeling smooth will mean forearm and hand light with top arm staying down, maintaining level when it is not taking the key-drop for the first and last tone; and alternating action taking key-drop for the middle tones—extension for black keys, and flexion for white.

This pattern purposely avoids any consecutive white keys. If the musical idea which is to be fixed needs a longer rhythmic line (more tones involved), simply play around inside of the rim tones, using a meter identical with the difficulty which is to be solved.

1. It is the sensation of easy smooth progression which is the value of this pattern.
2. It is that particular sensation which is to be transferred.
3. It is the *blend* in action, easily used in this pattern, which will solve the difficulties in the context to which it is transferred.
4. Only a fundamental rhythm creates a smooth blend.
5. Technical difficulties are the result of disrupting that blend.
6. These difficulties are always the result of over-using small muscles and under-using the larger muscles.
7. More than any other reason, this unbalance is created by reaching for the key with the fingers. Next in line is producing too much power for tone with the fingers.

One successful experience in transferring the chromatic octave pattern (its sensation of progression) to a stubborn difficulty and having the difficulty disappear is more illuminating than any amount of talk. It can prove in a moment that difficulties are solved by smooth rhythmic progression and not by hours of drill. This experience can be achieved through the use of this pattern.

The reason for this pattern's efficiency is that it uses a repeated action and "techniques other than fingers." The alternating action is natural for tucking in tones, and thus a note-wise procedure is easily avoided with the pattern.

Note-wise procedure must be avoided for success with any kind of difficulty. Learn to note the difference in the feeling in certain parts of a composition; also the difference in feeling in two varieties of Etudes. Superimpose the smoother variety of progression onto the troublesome one. For instance, try transferring the feeling of the Chopin Etude in sixths to the Etude in thirds. They do not feel alike as a rule in their early stages. One will feel easier than the other. Make the less easy one learn from the easy sensation.

This process of seeking a sensation which uses an easy flow of power and then letting that smooth flow solve difficulties which arise, is endless. The wonderful part of it is that there are always such places to be found and used. They can form a chain of accomplishments not duplicated, in the quality of the result or the ease with which it is achieved, by any other manner of practicing.

A transfer of sensation from teacher to pupil is also a means of solving problems expeditiously.

Here again is a field for learning which is largely unexplored and it is vastly more effective and efficient than explaining with words. Why not explain with the actual sensation of what is involved in playing with a smooth rhythmic follow-through? There is no answer except that traditional teaching has not emphasized this way of getting results. It has stressed the development of independence in controls, rather than a rhythmic follow-through with its necessary blended action of all the levers involved.

Added to the weight of tradition is the fact that a gifted aural learner wants to pay attention to how the music sounds, not to how it feels to produce it. He believes in his ears and is sure that if he knows exactly how it should sound, he can reproduce it.

He is completely right. He should never have to do anything

but listen, and this would be the case were it not for faulty habits of production—faulty in the fact that there is too much strain in producing power. When there are these faulty habits, there is no way out in correcting them but to pay attention to how it feels as the pupil plays—listening for effects will not suffice to correct old habits and establish new ones.

Then too there is a creative power in the physical rhythm which unquestionably influences the listening habits. When there is strain in production, this rhythm suffers and along with it the deepest insight for creating beauty with the music. Not until a rhythm begins to work, as yeast works in bread, does the whole learning change and ideas flourish.

The transferring of a sensation of this rhythm from teacher to pupil is perfectly possible. The success in this kind of teaching hinges on two things: the skill of the teacher in manipulating this transfer of sensation, and the rightness of his own body in using a rhythm. Of course, to be skilled in transferring this rhythm the teacher must have a vivid consciousness of what is involved in the total output as he plays—a necessary asset for being a teacher. Every teacher will use and develop his own best abilities in his approach for getting results. It has been my experience that this particular phase of teaching—transferring a sensation—which saves endless talk and goes straight to the difficulty being dealt with, is the phase of teaching which is the least adopted by my teacher-pupils. Yet they have all profited in establishing new physical habits as much or more by this phase of the teaching than by any other.

A teaching technique of superimposing a sensation of rhythmic activity is simply a development and extension of the manner in which a rhythmic transfer takes place from teacher to pupil in duet playing. There is the contact of the shoulders and arms, and with this contact it is no easier for a pupil to be "out of step" than it would be in dancing.

This simple example of duet playing demands very little of the teacher. But suppose he desires to give the sensation of the relationship of parts in the whole playing mechanism—the relationship of articulation to a fundamental rhythm. This means he must find a way of controlling movements temporarily, the activity of the pupil—activity from chair seat to fingers inclusive.

My manner of transferring the sensation is to slip my fingers between the fingers of the pupil while sitting close by. Instantly I can check on any reaching of his fingers, a down pressure in hand or forearm which should not be there, and know what the whole playing mechanism intends to do. The relationship of top arm staying down, while the forearm and hand stay tipped up and light can be made a definite sensation. Synchronizing all the activity with the music is important. Humming the phrase as the sensations are given easily does this. With the close relationship, the teacher can feel muscular activity as it takes place in the pupil. He can know when the fingers dive down to get to tone rather than being a part of a control started farther back. He can indicate finger activity by simply making slight movements with his own fingers against the pupil's hand.

Nothing can prove more conclusively to the pupil that he does reach with fingers than to be balked as he reaches. This is a vivid experience and makes the learning definite.

Forcing an octave span in the palm of the pupil is a thousand times more effective than saying that it should be between the second joint of the thumb and the hand knuckle joint of the little finger.

There are endless ways and means of effecting a transfer of sensation from teacher to pupil. The need of the moment creates the means. The need is *always* discovered by a musical lack in the pupil's performance. No diagnosis is ever valid unless it is made to correct a musical deficiency. It should always be the ear and not the eye of the teacher which finds fault with a performance. The eye can certainly corroborate what the ear has detected.

Assistance from the teacher for improving the way the music

sounds is the only right approach for assistance to technical difficulties. If the music really glows there are no unsolved technical difficulties. In that event, there is always a masterful rhythm at the helm of the physical coordination.

Learning with a rhythm will mean becoming skilled in sensing the important tones which build up the musical form. Resolving a composition into a regular and simple meter is one way. Pulsing and outlining is another.

The Bach Prelude in C minor is a perfect vehicle for pointing up the use of simple regularity for making more complicated playing easy:

Ill. 14

By the procedure outlined below, this Prelude has been taught to an adult who had never played the piano before. It was the rhythm as the counterpart of the aural image which turned the trick. No attempt was made to clear the reading process; ears and rhythm were the only factors needed to make a first contact with the instrument a musical experience.

It is one of my delights to teach this little Prelude at a first lesson with an actual beginner—true, an adult beginner, but nevertheless a beginner with no former experience in playing the piano. I do not have the pleasure of teaching many real beginners, for I no longer teach children; but when an adult beginner does come he gets this little Prelude—and I revel in having it provide his first contact with beautiful music.

Naturally the playing is done by rote, and if the ear is not quick, one measure will suffice to set the coordination working. There is no involvement with anything on the page; there is only the C-minor triad to be found on the keyboard. This is the way it sounds reduced to its simplest rhythmic pattern:

Pattern 9

I sit close by so that the swing of my torso contacts the right arm of the pupil. I begin rocking in each chord on the upper register of the keyboard. By rocking I mean the exaggeration of the swing of the torso and paying no attention to the action of articulation. The rock is exaggerated until it is taken over by the pupil, and then it is diminished to a very small but inevitable swing from side to side. As the rhythm of the sway grooves in with the sound of the triad as I play it, a synchronization begins to take place with the pupil, and one hand or the other is able to contact the triad—not every time with the regularity of the swing, but now and then. All the time I am rocking and playing the triad, I make it clear that I have no interest in anything except that the rhythm will contact the triad. The aural image has already been made accurate; the trouble at this point is the coordination of the playing mechanism as a whole.

The playing of the simple triad need involve nothing but spacing three bones—three fingers—and a swing against these bones. That can be achieved at the first lesson. When it is achieved, and the rhythm goes on and on contacting the triads regardless of what I say or do on the top register of the piano, I begin opening the triads and play the Prelude as Bach wrote it. Thus the aural image is refreshed, to be used at a second lesson. Of course the first contact of a pupil with the Prelude must be an emotional performance of it by the teacher. The pupil should always know, by having heard the composition, what it is that he is going to work with.

Naturally I chose this Prelude because of the similarity of the material in both hands and the consistency of the rhythmic pattern. Teaching the first two measures to the pupil gives him access to the whole Prelude, except for the next to last measure. Again at the second lesson we start with the pattern and play just the triads by the same process of rocking them into sound. Then I open the triad of the first quarter in the right hand (Pattern 10). Always one rhythmic irregularity at a time is absorbed into regularity—a fundamental procedure. But never any stopping. Remember—always take irregularities on the way to the regular beat. The attention is never directed either to the movements for articulation or the details of the rhythmic pattern, but to the fact that the larger regular beat is absorbing a detail—on the way.

The difficulty in opening the first triad varies, of course, with the individual. It is very difficult for some of the adults not to mind fumbling; they are apt to feel that they should be able to do it on a first try. But relentlessly I keep the rhythm going and insist that only the large rhythm matters; and after a time they can follow the leader. Maybe five minutes, maybe ten, maybe longer if they have been playing the regular chords while I have been opening the first beat of the pattern. (The pattern simply indicates the procedure; it does not give the number of repetitions necessary for achievement.) Also, simply keeping a regular rhythm going with the playing of a triad demands real concentration and is therefore fatiguing. Never try to cope with fatigue. Let the student be fresh for a first impression when opening the pattern.

When the opening of the first beat is achieved, then open the third beat in the left hand; but do not ask for the first beat to be opened at the same time—let it revert to the simple triad. One thing at a time, and that done easily, means a faster approach to the ultimate performance than allowing a feeling of uncertainty to creep into the rhythm, because complications are added too rapidly. I believe in tackling a complicated pattern but in reducing it to utter rhythmic simplicity; and then adding step by step the complexities. I am convinced that by this procedure progress in establishing the necessary coordinations for playing is much more rapid than when beginning at the beginning means one tone at a time in a very simple context. Please note that this statement refers to the physical coordination—not to establishing the aural image.

Now we have supposedly the first and third beats opened (without the two 16ths in the right hand) inside the simple regularity we started with. There remains the second beat to open and then the achievement of all three beats opened in sequence, without dissipating the feeling of the first approach to the Prelude. Teach the second beat opened as a follow-through of the first beat, which it is. Remember that the opening has been anticipated by its frequent repetition on the top part of the keyboard; the pattern has been heard and felt rhythmically before the actual playing of it is asked for. Discontinue the opening of the left hand third beat (simply play the triad) while the two first beats of the right hand are opened. Also, do not ask for consecutive openings. Let the rhythmic triad pattern have full sway the moment there is a slight confusion. Revert to it frequently in its simplest form; that means giving the pupil a chance to enjoy the rhythmic feeling of the Prelude—and that is very important. Never destroy that feeling. It is the major general of the whole operation. It will become the five star general of all future coordination if it is allowed to grow firm roots.

Achieving the playing of this little Prelude by a beginner in this manner has involved the fundamentals of all future accomplishment. The 16ths of the third beat in the right hand which complicate the physical coordination are played only when the pupil has become so accustomed to hearing them that he eventually plays them without actually being particularly aware that he has tucked them in.

First impressions have been linked with first things in importance; and the first plank of all future complicated coordinations has been put down. It will not need to be taken up or replaced in order, at some future time, to play a Beethoven Sonata with mastery.

Some way must be found to practice *for* performance at the outset, not after habits unrelated to a performance have been established. *Not stopping* a rhythmic procedure to the end is a demand for any exciting performance. It must be practiced first, for first habits can easily persist.

Actual playing involves the exact reverse of stopping. Why then practice stopping? Why not practice the fundamental requirement of a beautiful performance? This stopping for a faulty tone is one of the deadly sins established when a faulty tone is made more important than a going rhythm. See to it that the aural image is accurate; but also see to it that a going rhythm is more important in your piano playing life than a faulty tone. It is a matter of *which* is more important: a slip in the production of tone, or the disruption of the rhythm. A performance is not too greatly marred by a faulty tone, but it is ruined by a faulty halting rhythm. Even the chance of 100 percent accuracy is enhanced enormously when a going rhythm is used as the only adequate projector of the aural image.

PULSING

Pulsing is one of the means of practicing a going rhythm. Call it outlining, scanning—what you will. Pulsing suggests a live physical activity, and for that reason more nearly fits the bill. It is simply a means of approaching a composition that intensifies the musically important tones. For that reason it is a valuable tonic that builds up a rhythmic foundation. Anything that nullifies note-wise playing is to be cherished and consistently used.

To be effective, the first requisite is that pulsing should intensify and not cancel the emotional reaction to the music. No reading that is simply a matter of reading all the notes without feeling the beauty of the music should ever be tolerated. First impressions are too important for that. They must deal with the all-important factor—the musical idea.

Pulsing is a means of *feeling* the music—nothing else. By leaving out passing tones and modifiers, it highlights the tones left in. It is these tones that should have a direct sequence in rhythmic progression, an intense reaction to form.

Just how necessary an awareness of form is for projecting a musical idea is exhibited every day in the concert field. There are those performers who are meticulous in playing every note on the page with clarity, but who never succeed in projecting a musical idea with simplicity and beauty. Then there is the artist who deals with nothing that clutters the clarity of the musical idea. With him the listener is never at a loss in hearing the basic musical progression.

Pulsing is a device for stressing the projection of the musical idea. It succeeds because it intensifies the relationship of important tones. It does so simply by omitting all the tones that can be left out without damaging the clarity of the musical statement.

Omitting tones is the negative side of the picture. Just leaving out a number of tones is no good; than can mean a zero in finding the musical idea. Pulsing must be a reading that instinctively goes to the important tones and creates with those tones a starkly simple but beautiful line of musical progression.

It must involve the emotional reaction to the music. When this happens, pulsing helps develop a keen observation of the structural form and associates the emotional reaction to the music primarily with that form.

This is a highly desirable state of affairs. It increases an awareness of the manner in which details contribute to form, without cluttering it up. For only when form is clearly etched can details assume their own rightful contribution to the beauty of the composition as a whole.

These means of learning with a rhythm have been used—with thrills and excitement and success. Exploring with a rhythm is an endless delight. There is never any danger of trusting it too much as a sure means for creating all the beauty which the ear is capable of imaging.

We leave it without a double bar, knowing that there is no final cadence to the theme of learning with a rhythm.

Index

Absolute pitch, 6
Accuracy, 54, 55, 103, 104
Action
    alternating, 28, 39, 40, 45, 74,
        80, 88, 96, 102, 114, 138
    arm, 85
    balance of, 97
    continuity of, 20, 33
    down, 39, 41
    finger, 41, 49, 94, 118
    forearm, 41, 44, 45
    hand, 45, 47, 48
    horizontal, 9, 20, 21, 113, 133
    individualized, 53, 54
    key, 67, 85
    repeated, 6, 29, 40, 47, 73, 78–
        81, 83, 87–95, 102, 137
    rotary, 42, 44, 45, 53, 54, 73,
        80, 87, 91, 93–96, 111, 114,
        117, 122
    sidewise, 71
    specific, explanation of terms, 24–
        29
    timing of, 11, 12
    up, 52, 53
    vertical, 9, 20, 21, 45, 73, 108

Activity, 7–9
    center of radius of, 26, 33, 42
    in torso and arms, 23, 24
Adult beginner, 141
Alternating action, 28, 39, 40, 45,
    74, 80, 88, 96, 102, 114, 138
Analysis of playing mechanism
    as related to use of distance, 67–
    75
    as related to use of power plus
        distance, 76–124
Arm (*see also* Forearm, Full arm,
    Top arm)
    action, 85
    in distance, 67–75
    in power plus distance, 76–124
    statement of activity, 23, 24
    weight of, 54
Arpeggios, 44, 51, 103–122
    problems and solutions, 105, 106,
        116–122
    factors in playing, 105, 111
    crucial point, 105
    analyzing pattern, 118–122
Articulation, 4–6, 26, 41, 52, 79,
    133

Sensation, 95
  transferring, 135, 138–140
Short notes, 130
Shostakovich
  Prelude, Op. 34, No. 15, 89
Shoulders, 16, 26, 29, 44, 67, 74,
  111, 112, 116
Sidewise action, 71
Sidewise play, 71
Sight reading, 7, 14
Sixths, 96
Skating, 8, 19, 20, 31
Skips, 70, 72
Slow practice, 54
Smallest musical unit, 26
Snap, 28, 29, 91, 92
"Snugging up," 103
Soft pedal, 64
Solo concert, 12, 13
Spacing, 11, 12
Span
  octave, 97–99
  of time, 20
Specific Action
  explanation of terms, 24–29
Speed, 54, 55, 74, 78
Spine, 32
Sports, 11, 12, 36
  See also Skating
Staccato, 21, 22, 52, 53
Staying down, 27
Stopping, 36, 145
String quartets, 58
Stroke, full arm, 36
Sustaining pedal, 64
Synchronization of controls, 35

Teaching, 5, 11, 31
  methods (traditional), 46–58
Techniques other than with fingers,
  30–45
Telescope, 68, 69
Tempo, 134
Terms
  explanation of, used in relation
    to a specific action, 24–29
Throw, 28, 29, 74
Throwing of hand, 115
Thumb, 24, 26, 29, 110, 113
  in horizontal distance, 68–72

  in in-and-out distance, 74, 75
  in octaves, 98, 99
  in passing, 42–45
  in vertical distance, 72–73
Time, span of, 20
Time values, 56, 128–131
Timing, 7, 19, 36, 42, 107
  of action, 11, 12
Tonal relationships, 128–131
Tone
  production, 18, 19, 21, 27, 33–
    37, 40, 48, 49, 60, 72, 77
  quality, 18, 19, 52
Tone-wise listening, 87
Top arm, 8, 11, 14, 16, 20, 26–28,
  54, 60
  in arpeggios, 103–122
  in distance, 67–75
  in double notes, 96, 97
  in learning with a rhythm, 126,
    127, 134, 136
  in octaves, 97–103
  in power plus distance, 76–124
  in repeated action, 78–81
  in scales, 123, 124
  in techniques other than with
    fingers, 32–39, 44, 45
  in trills, 81–95
Torso, 8, 9, 11, 14–16, 20, 26, 27,
  60
  in distance, 68, 69, 72
  in learning with a rhythm, 126,
    127, 134, 136, 142
  in power plus distance, 77, 78, 86
  in techniques other than with
    fingers, 31–33, 37
  statement of activity in, 23, 24
Toscanini, 13, 14
"Touch," 52
Transferring a sensation, 135, 138–
  140
Transposition, 62, 63
Traveling, 27
Tremolo, 73
Trills
  double thirds, 95
  octave, 81–88
  single, 88–94
  violinist's, 94
Tucked in, 29, 135, 136, 138